Beginnings, Middles and Ends

*Peter Hudson
and David Halls*

GW00708149

SPHERE BOOKS LIMITED

SPHERE BOOKS LTD

Published by the Penguin Group
27 Wrights Lane, London W8 5TZ, England
Viking Penguin Inc., 40 West 23rd Street, New York, New York 10010, USA
Penguin Books Australia Ltd, Ringwood, Victoria, Australia
Penguin Books Canada Ltd, 2801 John Street, Markham, Ontario, Canada L3R 1B4
Penguin Books (NZ) Ltd, 182–190 Wairau Road, Auckland 10, New Zealand

Penguin Books Ltd, Registered Offices: Harmondsworth, Middlesex, England

First published in Great Britain by Sphere Books Ltd, 1988
Copyright © 1988 by Peter Hudson and David Halls

Index compiled by Peva Keane

Printed and bound in Great Britain by
Richard Clay Ltd, Bungay, Suffolk

CONTENTS

Middles

Ends

FOREWORD

To follow fads and fashions in food has never really been our bag. However we do experiment with new things as they come along and try different dishes when we travel.

Food to us should be something not too difficult to put together, not too expensive (except when you really want to go mad), not too time consuming, *but*, it must have quality and a definite end result. That is, a dish that looks appealing, smells wonderful . . . and tastes great.

Too often food writers create new dishes or fads, purely for the sake of creating them. We have never subscribed to that theory. We prefer to analyse and change favourite dishes that we have cooked over the last two decades, and up-date them if required, or if they still have the old appeal . . . leave well alone! Neither do we subscribe to spending a fortune trying to obtain ingredients that are currently out of season . . . nature has her reasons!

As an example, take asparagus. We wait for it to appear in the shops each year, then indulge ourselves nearly every day. Tinned or frozen can never match the exquisite colour and taste of freshly cooked spears, but serve the purpose for some casseroles and soups. Anyway, we are sure or moderately sure, that if you indulged yourself with caviar and champagne everyday, you would become bored.

We do change our diet around quite a bit by alternating new, lighter-type dishes with the old basics. When we feel our palate is jaded, something Chinese or Italian quickly brings us back to the land of the living. In other words our tastes are very catholic and we believe variety really is the spice of life!

By breaking this particular collection into 'beginnings, middles and ends', we want you to delve into each section as the mood takes you.

The 'beginnings' may seem few, but we often have a delicious mixed or green salad to begin a meal. They provide a fresh clean taste and help to cut back on over-indulging, when it comes to the 'middle' course.

Likewise, end a meal with fresh cheese and fruit instead of a dessert.

Over the years, one of the things we always make sure we have to hand, is good homemade stock. Commercial stocks can certainly be used (and there are some excellent ones on the market), however, there is a difference in the final outcome of the dish. The same applies with wine used . . . the better the wine the better the flavour of the dish.

When browsing through these recipes, don't discard things like stuffed squid, Sichuan beef and bean curd, Avocado pie. They are not there so that some reviewer can pick them out and call us 'slightly trendy', they are there because they are superb dishes that we use frequently and are different and flavoursome.

If you only used this book to master the superb, tender crêpes, then it will have been worth it!

NOTE ON MEASUREMENTS

Where cups are used to measure ingredients, a set of standard measuring cups should be used, in which 1 cup holds 250 mls and 4 cups = 1 litre.

Beginnings

CREAM OF BEETROOT SOUP
Serves 4

This is nothing like Bortsch. We use fresh tender beetroot, not large ones, to achieve the best results, although canned beetroot can be used quite successfully providing it is packed in water and not vinegar. As with many vegetable soups, this is rather nice sprinkled with some small croutons and freshly chopped chives. For the ready prepared mustard part, you can choose Dijon, German or even an English mustard but it would be a mistake to use ones where a lot of vinegar has been used in their preparation.

> 1 medium onion, finely chopped
> 2 cloves garlic, crushed
> 2 tablespoons butter
> 1 tablespoon plain flour
> 3 cups well-flavoured home-made chicken stock
> Freshly ground black pepper
> 1 teaspoon red wine vinegar
> 425 grams (15 oz) cooked beetroot peeled and chopped
> $\frac{1}{2}$ to 1 teaspoon of prepared mustard
> 1 tablespoon arrowroot
> $\frac{1}{4}$ cup of cream

Sauté the onion and garlic in the butter over a low heat in a heavy-based largish pan with a lid. Keep

the lid on and cook the onions and garlic until soft
but not coloured for about 7 to 10 minutes. Add the
plain flour and cook, stirring all the while for about
a minute. Pour in the chicken stock and bring to
the boil while still stirring. Add the vinegar, some
pepper and the beetroot, lower the heat and gently
simmer covered for about 20 minutes. Take off the
heat and cool slightly, then purée in a food processor
until smooth. Return to the rinsed out saucepan,
add the mustard and then check for seasoning. Mix
the arrowroot with a little cold water, then add the
cream and pour into the soup. Bring back to the
boil, stirring all the time and simmer for 2 minutes.
Serve in warm soup bowls or soup plates.

CREAM OF CAULIFLOWER SOUP
Serves 4–6

As this soup attains a creamy texture in the food
processor, it is not really necessary to thicken it.
However, the addition of about a tablespoon of
arrowroot mixture with a little water and added at
the last few minutes of cooking helps to bind the
soup together and gives it an even creamier texture.
Also you may wish to swirl in about a tablespoon of
butter for extra flavour. Good home-made chicken
stock is essential to the finished flavour of this particular soup; it is not a good idea to use instant
stock cubes. If you really like the taste of cauliflower
we suggest that you save cauliflower cooking water
and add to the soup in equal quantities with the

chicken stock. Should you favour a blander taste, then use all chicken stock, and half cream half milk at the end, as cream added to any soup reduces and smoothes out the flavour. It depends on your own personal taste and diet of course.

> 1 medium sized cauliflower
> 1 teaspoon of salt
> 1 cup reserved cauliflower water ⎱ or 2 cups
> 1 cup home-made chicken stock ⎰ chicken stock
> Freshly ground black pepper
> Freshly grated nutmeg to taste
> 1 cup milk (or ½ cup milk, ½ cup cream)
> 1 scant tablespoon arrowroot mixed with a little
>   water (optional)
> A tablespoon of butter (optional)

Wash the cauliflower and break into florets. Place in a large pan and cover with water together with a teaspoon of salt. Bring to the boil, lower the heat and simmer until soft. Drain, reserving the cooking water. Either force the cooked cauliflower through a sieve or place in a food processor and process together with the 2 cups of liquid of your choice (either reserved cooking water and stock or all stock) until the mixture is smooth. Put back in the rinsed-out pan and reheat gently. Season with pepper and nutmeg to taste and add milk (or milk and cream). Thicken if desired with the arrowroot and water. Heat thoroughly and if liked stir in 1 tablespoonful of butter to enrich the flavour just before serving.

WATERCRESS SOUP
Serves 4

As watercress is available through most of the year you will be able to make this often. This recipe has two recommendations: one, it is so easy and tasty and two, watercress contains a lot of iron and is a good way of getting that mineral into the diet. The five cups of slightly salted water mentioned below contain only one teaspoon of salt between them. Should you be on a salt-free diet or wish to cut down on your salt intake, you can use your own home-made de-fatted chicken stock or alternatively leave out the salt altogether and at the very end when you are about to serve, sprinkle over some lemon juice to sharpen the soup a little.

> 1 tablespoon of butter or vegetable oil
> A large bunch of watercress, coarsely chopped (reserve about 2 dozen leaves for later)
> 5 cups lightly salted water
> 4 medium-sized potatoes, peeled and sliced
> A few gratings of fresh nutmeg
> Salt and freshly ground pepper to taste
> $\frac{1}{4}$ cup cream
> 2 egg yolks

Heat the butter or oil in a large heavy-based pot and add the coarsely chopped watercress and sauté for about 5 minutes until softened. Add the five cups of salted water and the sliced potatoes and simmer for about 20 minutes once the water has come to the boil, or until the potatoes are soft. Place in a food processor and process until thoroughly smooth. Return to the rinsed-out pot and bring back to simmering point. Season with the nutmeg, salt and pepper as desired and then add the reserved watercress leaves. Meanwhile, in a small bowl beat together the cream and the egg yolks. Stir into this mixture a few tablespoons of the hot soup and mix well. Take the soup off the heat source and stir in the egg and cream mixture and mix well. Add a lump of butter to enrich the flavour further and serve immediately.

NOTE It will not be an injustice to the soup if you do not add the cream and egg-yolk mixture as the soup should be sufficiently thick because of the inclusion of the potatoes. However, a lump of butter stirred in at the end, about a tablespoonful, does give the soup a richer flavour, and you have only used two tablespoons for the whole recipe for four people so that can hardly be called going over the top. Or you can substitute half water and half milk for the cream and egg yolk mixture if you wish.

COLD CITRUS SOUP
Serves 4–6

Terribly refreshing and different without being too way out, is how we would describe this soup. It's a very reasonable dish in terms of cost most of the year, especially if you have the fruits growing in your own garden, as we do. To give it a slight difference when you serve it, try adding a teaspoon of pernod to each serving just prior to presenting it at table. Should the gelatin set into too stiff a jelly, just break it up when you spoon it into some tall glasses. We prefer a mixture of the grapefruit and oranges rather than just one or the other, but the choice is yours. We must stress, however, that the best result is obtained by the use of *fresh* orange juice and not bottled or canned.

> 2 to 3 large ripe grapefruit or oranges (or a
>   mixture of both)
> 1 level tablespoon gelatin powder
> 2 cups fresh orange juice
> 3 tablespoons sugar
> 3 tablespoons fresh lime juice
> Mint sprigs to decorate if needed

Cut all the peel including the white pith from the fruit; do this over a bowl so as to catch any juices. Section the fruit with a sharp knife, removing any pips and membrane. Keep several whole sections of fruit aside for decoration, then cut the remainder into bite-sized pieces and place in a bowl. Make up the juices in the bowl to half a cup with extra fresh orange juice and place in a small saucepan. Sprinkle the gelatin powder over and leave for 10 minutes. Gently heat the gelatin and juice, stirring all the time until the gelatin has dissolved; do not let the mixture boil. Take off the heat and mix in the sugar until dissolved, then add the remaining orange juice and lime juice. Leave to cool and pour over the bite-sized pieces of fruit. Chill for at least 4 hours. Serve in chilled glasses or bowls. Decorate with the reserved fruit slices and some sprigs of mint, and pernod if desired.

NOTE If you decide to make this with all grapefruit, omit the fresh lime juice, add a little extra sugar to taste, and add just a few drops of angostura bitters, instead of pernod, to the orange juice and gelatin mixture once it has cooled down. We have said that it will feed 4–6 because only a little is needed to stimulate the appetite prior to a middle course.

CHILLED CUCUMBER AND MINT SOUP
Serves 4

Not only is this a pleasant cooling soup for warmer weather, it is also ideal to begin a meal that might have a heavy or rich middle course to follow. When the weather is really hot, consider serving this in well-chilled bowls or serve in a large bowl or dish set into a larger bowl of cracked ice. You might also like to add to it some slices of ripe avocado that have been dipped into some lemon juice; it is also good with the addition of a few chilled cooked prawns or shrimps. Try using some of the varieties of mint in the garden such as applemint or pineapple mint.

> *2 tablespoons of butter or vegetable oil*
> *2 cups of peeled and seeded cucumber*
> *2 leeks, white part only, sliced*

> *2 cups home-made chicken stock*
> *1 teaspoon lemon juice, or more to taste if you wish*
> *1 large bayleaf*
> *A minimum of 2 tablespoons of chopped mint*
> *Salt and freshly ground white pepper to taste*
> *¾ cup cream, sour cream or half cream half milk*

In a large pot heat the butter or oil and add the cucumber and leeks. Cover and cook gently for 5 minutes without allowing them to brown. Add the stock, lemon juice, bayleaf and mint. Bring to the boil, lower the heat and simmer very gently for 15 to 20 minutes. Leave to cool slightly. Remove bayleaf and place in a food processor. Process until smooth. Place in a bowl, season lightly and add the cream, sour cream or half-milk half-cream mixture. Stir well and when cooled right down, cover and keep in the fridge until really cold. To serve, decorate with thin slices of fresh cucumber and sprigs of mint.

COLD AVOCADO SOUP
Serves 6

We make no apologies for including this as it is one of our favourites. It does seem such a pity to mash up avocado in this way but it is an ideal way to begin a plain simple meal because it is so easy to prepare. We have used avocados that were a little sunburnt – it is true; they do get their skins burnt by too much sun! They are the ones that have a hard piece of flesh under the surface of the discoloured skin. If you do use these, because sometimes they are sold cheaply, then make sure that you only use the perfect part of the flesh and not any of the discoloured portion, in which case you will need possibly four or five for this dish.

> 3 ripe avocado (or up to 5 if sunburnt)
> 2 cups home-made well-flavoured chicken stock
> 1 cup cream
> 1 cup sour cream
> Few drops tabasco
> A little salt and white pepper
> 1 teaspoon avocado oil (if available)
> Juice of half a lemon, or to taste
> 1 tablespoon dry vermouth

If you have a large food processor place the flesh of the avocado together with the remaining ingredients and process until smooth. You may have to stop the machine and scrape down the side of the bowl. If it is a small processor do in two batches and mix together in a glass bowl. When blended, cover and chill for several hours prior to serving.

NOTE We have mentioned adding avocado oil; this can be obtained from good delicatessens or through some healthfood shops. It is not essential, but it does give it an extra roundness of flavour. We also use the oil, combined with another lighter oil, sometimes when making salad dressings.

CRÊPE CAKE
Serves 4–6

This is a simple dish to make, especially if you have
a batch of ready-made crêpes in the freezer. The
fillings given in this recipe to use between the crêpes
can be varied to suit your own taste. Some form of
green vegetable, here we use lettuce, moistened with
a little béchamel sauce, is essential to the finished
dish. You could use spinach, chard or silverbeet or
even some shredded cabbage, in which case they
should be blanched first to soften them. Instead of
cooked chicken or Bolognese sauce you could use
cooked left-over fish or smoked fish, canned fish if
nothing else is available, or perhaps turkey or ham.
The cheese is essential in every case, as it not only
adds flavour and protein but also helps to bind the
layers together when it is baked in the oven. We
will give you our foolproof, thin, tender crêpe recipe
which will make about 25 crêpes the size of a normal
crêpe pan. When cooked and cooled they can be
stacked between greaseproof paper: we do six together and then paper between every six. Well wrap
or bag, making sure you exclude as much air as
possible and freeze flat for later use. When they are
to be used let the crêpes thaw down at room temperature; or you can thaw briefly in a microwave
oven at 30 per cent power for about 4–5 minutes,
turning the package of six over once during that
time.

Basic Crêpe Recipe

2 cups plain flour
2 cups milk
4 large eggs
150 grams (5 oz) melted butter
Pinch salt (optional)

Sift flour and salt, if used, into a large mixing bowl.
Mix in the eggs and the milk and beat thoroughly,
using a rotary whisk, hand whisk or electric beater
to get rid of any lumps. Add the cooled melted butter
and again mix well. Then leave the mixture to stand
for 1 hour, when the mixture should be like thin
cream; if it is a little too thick, thin down slightly
with some water. When you come to cook the crêpes
make sure that you have ready a good medium-
sized crêpe pan. We have one that is used for making
either crêpes or omelets and nothing else, and is
never *washed*. After each use the pan is wiped out
with some paper towelling. There are pans on the
market that are coated with a non-stick surface,
and are ideal for the making of crêpes. Whichever
pan you use, lightly coat it inside with a little
clarified butter or vegetable oil and heat it up to
fairly hot. Pour only enough of the crêpe batter into
the pan to just coat the bottom when you have
swirled the batter around. For judging this we have
a ladle, which we again keep for this purpose as it
contains exactly the right amount for one crêpe
(generally you will find each crêpe needs about a
scant ¼ cup or even down to ⅓ cup).

Keep the crêpe mixture in the pan to the

minimum, for crêpes should be thin, not like a thick pancake – there is a difference. Cook until the top surface of the crêpe loses its wet appearance, turn either by flipping or with a broad spatula and cook on the other side for about 1 minute. Remove to a plate to cool. After you have made your first crêpe you can then adjust the cooking surface either up or down, depending on how the first one turned out. The colour you are looking for is a deep beige to brown surface on either side but certainly not burnt. Stack the crêpes on a plate as you cook them. These may be stored in the fridge for several days either covered with clingwrap or foil to retain their moisture, or well wrapped and frozen for later use. You can also make these in a food processor. Place the milk and eggs into the processor, add the flour and salt and process until smooth; you may have to scrape the sides of the processor bowl down once. With the motor running, pour the cooled melted butter through the feed tube on to the mixture and continue to process until well blended. Tip out into a bowl and leave to stand for 1 hour, then check the consistency, if necessary adding extra liquid to thin the mixture down prior to making the crêpes. You will also need for the Crêpe Cake a recipe for quick Béchamel sauce which we will include here.

NOTE To make a wholemeal crêpe we suggest you use 1 cup of fine wholemeal flour and 1 cup plain flour or buckwheat flour and plain flour. In our particular recipe, using either all wholemeal or all buckwheat is not very successful in conjunction with the quantities of the other ingredients.

Quick Béchamel Sauce

> 1 tablespoon butter
> 2 tablespoons plain flour
> 1 cup milk
> 1 large bayleaf
> A pinch each of freshly grated nutmeg, salt and white pepper

Melt the butter in a heavy-based saucepan and blend in the flour. Add all the milk and whisk until the mixture starts to simmer. Add the rest of the ingredients and cook slowly stirring all the time for about 5 minutes or until the raw taste of the flour has disappeared. Cool. If it should go lumpy, beat with a whisk until smooth.

Crêpe Fillings

> $\frac{1}{2}$ a large or 1 small compact lettuce
> 2 cups cooked chicken, chopped small or left-over Bolognese sauce
> 4 to 6 good tablespoons of tomato paste
> 1 cup of grated Cheddar cheese

Boil the lettuce for 5 minutes in enough water to cover and to which you have added one teaspoon of sugar. Drain, cool and squeeze dry, then chop up fairly finely. Mix with 4 good tablespoons of cooled béchamel sauce. Add the same amount of béchamel to the cooked chicken or Bolognese sauce. Heat the oven to Gas Mark 6 (400°F, 200°C). Place one crêpe on a heatproof serving dish. Cover with a thin layer of the lettuce mixture and sprinkle over a little grated cheese. Place another crêpe on top and cover with a little of the meat mixture. Another crêpe and then a thin layer of the tomato paste. Continue layering with crêpes and fillings in the same order until the fillings are used. Top with a crêpe and add any remaining cheese to the remaining béchamel sauce and spread over the top. Brown in the oven for at least 15 minutes. Serve hot cut into wedges.

NOTE As this can slip sideways while cooking we suggest that you insert several long toothpicks into the cake at a slight angle before baking it in the oven. These can be either of wood or thin metal. However, do remove them before serving to your guests. As well as making a good beginning to a light meal the cake can also be served as a middle course accompanied with a mixed or green salad, followed by fresh fruit and a soft creamy cheese for dessert. As a main course it will only feed four people.

RUSSIAN CRÊPES
Serves 4

This simple dish is easily prepared and is ideal for the warmer weather. The crêpes can be made and filled in advance and kept covered in the fridge prior to serving time when you can put on the topping of sour cream and caviar or lumpfish roe. However, do make sure that they come back to almost room temperature before serving; if they are too cold they are not as pleasant to eat. The decoration can be as simple or as lavish as you yourself have the time or talent for. We usually lay the filled crêpes side by side on a fairly long serving dish and drizzle the stirred sour cream across the centre, then lay a line of caviar atop the sour cream so that only the centre of each crêpe is decorated. A batch of crêpes made with half buckwheat flour and plain flour are particularly good (see page 14).

> 8 cooked crêpes
> 1 cup of cottage cheese
> $\frac{1}{2}$ small onion, very finely chopped
> A little salt and black pepper if desired, or tabasco instead of pepper
> $\frac{1}{2}$–1 cup of sour cream, vigorously stirred to make it runny
> Small jar of caviar or red or black lumpfish roe

Mix the cottage cheese and onion together very well with a wooden spoon and season if desired. Divide this mixture equally down the centre of each crêpe and roll up fairly tightly and place on a serving plate. Spoon the runny sour cream across the centre of the crêpes and then spoon the caviar across the centre of the sour cream.

KIDNEY-FILLED CRÊPES
Serves 4

The same applies to kidneys as it does to liver: DO
NOT OVERCOOK, as the result will be tough. If you
have some cooked crêpes to hand, this will be a
relatively easy and quick dish to prepare. Assemble
all your ingredients before you start cooking. Also
have your lightly buttered heatproof serving dish
ready to place the filled crêpes into; and pre-heat
your oven.

> 4 large lamb kidneys
> 1 tablespoon of peanut oil or clarified butter
> 1 medium onion, very thinly sliced
> 2 ripe tomatoes skinned, seeded and chopped
> $\frac{1}{4}$ cup dry white wine
> 1 tablespoon finely chopped parsley
> $\frac{1}{2}$ teaspoon dried marjoram
> 2 tablespoons cream
> Freshly ground black pepper

Skin, core and thinly slice the kidneys. Heat the oil
or butter in a shallow heavy-based pan and sauté
the onion gently for about 3 minutes. Raise the
heat slightly and stir in the kidneys and cook,
stirring all the while, for a further 2 minutes. Add
the tomatoes, white wine, parsley and marjoram.
Bring quickly to the boil, then lower the heat and
simmer for 2 minutes more. Stir in the cream, season
with black pepper and remove the pan from the
heat. Using a slotted spoon, divide the mixture
equally between the crêpes and roll up. Place in the

buttered oven dish and bake at Gas Mark 4 (350°F, 180°C) for 15 minutes. Serve topped with any juices left from the pan and some extra chopped parsley.

NOTE Instead of the white wine you may use any of the following to ring the changes: dry or medium sherry, Sercial madeira or madeira, port or either sweet or dry vermouth. When you add the kidneys you can also add 1 tablespoon cognac or brandy.

CURRIED SEAFOOD CRÊPES
Serves 4

This is ideal as a beginning of a meal, especially if you have some cooked crêpes in your freezer. The addition of scallops and shrimps in the recipe enhances the fish flavour of the finished dish. Most firm, white, non-oily fish can be used; we generally use fillets of flounder or sole. To ring the changes, you might like to substitute for the shrimps either a small tin of crab meat or about 4 heaped tablespoons of smoked fish roe. In either case add them after you have removed the pan from the heat, having stirred in the cream or sour cream.

>   8 cooked crêpes
>   1 tablespoon butter
>   1 teaspoon good curry powder
>   2 small fish fillets, cubed
>   6 large scallops cut into thirds
>   1 dozen small shelled shrimps

1 tablespoon plain flour
¼ cup dry white wine
½ cup of fish or chicken stock
¼ cup cream or sour cream
Very little salt and pepper to taste (lemon juice optional)

Melt butter in a shallow pan and stir in the curry powder. Cook for 30 seconds to release the flavour. Add fish, scallops and shrimps and cook for one minute. Sprinkle over the flour and stir in quickly. Add wine, let it bubble and then pour in the stock. Stir and cook for 30 seconds. Lastly add cream or sour cream, stir several times and remove pan from heat. Leave to cool slightly. Check seasoning. Instead of salt and pepper try a little lemon juice. Butter a large flat ovenproof serving dish and, using a slotted spoon, divide the mixture evenly between the 8 crêpes. Roll each crêpe up and place side by side in the buttered dish. Spoon the remaining sauce in the pan over the rolled crêpes and bake until just warmed through in a pre-heated oven set at Gas Mark 3 (325°F, 170°C) for about 15 minutes.

BABY LEEKS IN YOGHURT SAUCE
Serves 4

The stress here is on small young leeks not the larger ones that you would use for stews or soups. Most people serve them cold with a vinaigrette sauce but by using this egg and yoghurt sauce you have a

more substantial dish with which to begin a meal.
The sauce is a little bit of extra work as you have to
take the time and patience to cook it in the top of a
double boiler. However, it is worth mastering as
you can use it with other things such as cold
poached fish or poached chicken breasts.

> 8 young thin leeks
> Juice of a large lemon
> Split clove of garlic
> ¼ teaspoon salt
> 1 teaspoon each of whole peppercorns and fennel
>   seeds
> 8 coriander seeds
> 6 sprigs parsley
> 3 spring onions, roughly chopped
> 1¼ cups plain yoghurt
> 3 large egg yolks
> 2 teaspoons lemon juice
> 2 teaspoons Dijon mustard

Clean and trim the leeks, leaving on about 2 inches
of the green part, and place in a single layer in a
large stovetop shallow dish preferably with a lid. If
the dish has no lid, cover with a double thickness of
foil to keep in the steam. In a fairly large pot place 3
cups of water together with the first amount of
lemon juice, garlic, salt, the peppercorn, fennel seed
and coriander spices, parsley and spring onions.
Cook this poaching liquid over a low heat for 10
minutes to make a well-flavoured stock. Strain the
stock over the leeks, cover as suggested and simmer
for about 15 minutes or until they are just cooked.

Leave to cool in the liquid. Beat the yoghurt, egg yolks and second amount of lemon juice in the top of the double boiler over simmering water (a bowl could be used here). Cook the sauce, stirring all the time until it thickens, about 15 minutes. Add the mustard. Take off the heat and leave the sauce to cool, stirring occasionally. Drain the leeks, and place on a serving dish with the sauce spooned over them.

HOT CUCUMBER WITH MUSHROOMS AND SHRIMPS
Serves 4

Most people seem to consider cucumber as a vegetable that is only served cold in or with some form of salad. This is one of the exceptions and it is really delicious. The long thin 'telegraph' variety is the best to use, but if unavailable almost any other kind will be suitable. If you want to make this dish in advance to re-heat later, you should make the filling and put it in an ovenproof serving dish. Sprinkle with a few chopped chives or dill and then cover with a thin layer of breadcrumbs, dot with butter and bake in a hot oven until the top is golden brown.

1 large cucumber
125 grams (4½ oz) button mushrooms, sliced
50 grams (2 oz) butter
1 tablespoon plain flour

$\frac{1}{2}$ *cup chicken stock*
$\frac{1}{2}$ *cup cream*
Freshly ground black pepper
1 teaspoon soy sauce
125 grams ($4\frac{1}{2}$ oz) shelled prawns or shrimp
1 spring onion, finely chopped.

Wash the cucumber and, leaving the skin on, dice into about $\frac{3}{4}$ inch cubes. Put in a pan of lightly salted water and simmer for 3 minutes, drain and refresh in cold water to stop the cooking process and set the colour. Drain again and leave to one side. Sauté the sliced mushrooms in the butter for a few minutes, add the drained cucumber and simmer, covered, over a low heat for a further 3 minutes. Sprinkle the flour over and mix thoroughly. Pour in the stock and cream, adding some black pepper and the soy sauce. Stir to mix while the mixture comes to the boil, lower the heat and add either the prawns, cut up, or the shrimps and heat through. Serve in small dishes immediately.

DUCK PÂTÉ USING PARTIALLY COOKED DUCK
Serves 8–10

This pâté is intended to be made using the remaining meat from the Duck Breasts In Pastry recipe that can be found in the 'Middles' section on page 116 of this book. Should you want to make this without using the other recipe first, then roast a good plump duck at Gas Mark 6 (400°F, 200°C) on a rack in a baking tin for 50 to 60 minutes and then leave to cool. As the duck meat has already been cooked this is not as rich as you might imagine, for the simple reason that most of the fat has been cooked out of it when roasted.

> Remaining meat from the two ducks (breasts already removed)
> or 1 plump duck (see above)
> 300 grams (11 oz) minced meat, beef, veal or lean pork
> ½ cup fresh white or wholemeal breadcrumbs
> Extra duck liver, minced (optional)
> 1 teaspoon dried chervil
> 2 tablespoons finely chopped parsley
> Grated rind of 1 orange
> 2 tablespoons brandy
> A little salt and freshly ground black pepper
> 2 small eggs, lightly beaten
> 3 rashers of fatty bacon
> 2 large bayleaves

Cut the meat from the ducks (or duck) and mince coarsely. Except for the bacon and bayleaves, add the other ingredients, binding with the eggs. Spoon into a well-buttered dish just large enough to hold the pâté. Lay the bacon rashers across the top and press on the two bayleaves. Cover with a double thickness of buttered foil and press well around the edges of the dish to seal in all the moisture while cooking. Bake in a roasting tin half filled with water at Gas Mark 3 (325°F, 170°C) for about 1–1¼ hours. Remove from the oven and place a weight on top until cold. We like this served with hot wholemeal toast and redcurrant jelly.

KIDNEYS IN GIN AND JUNIPER BERRY SAUCE
Serves 4

People tend to regard our recipes that have booze in them as exotic figments of our imagination. This is not true. Yes, we are known to have a tipple, but we rarely put alcohol into dishes just for the sake of it. We do it because there is a purpose for that alcohol. In recipes where the addition of alcohol is not always essential we put the word optional in brackets by the side of it. In this case it is essential to the final flavour of the dish; it also cuts down on the richness. We suggest that rather than serve the kidneys on a croute, you should serve them over a few spoonfuls of plain boiled rice.

> *12 lamb kidneys*
> *2 tablespoons clarified butter*
> *¼ cup gin*
> *10 juniper berries, crushed*
> *2 tablespoons finely chopped spring onion*
> *⅓ cup good chicken or veal stock*
> *2 tablespoons cold butter*
> *A little salt and freshly ground black pepper*
> *2 good teaspoons fresh lemon juice*

Remove the skins from the kidneys, cut in half lengthways and then cut out the white core (either poultry shears or kitchen scissors are best for this). Heat the clarified butter in a heavy-based frying-pan and sauté the kidneys over moderate heat, stirring them for about 2 minutes. Pour in the gin carefully and set alight. Shake the pan until the flames have died down, and with a slotted spoon remove the kidneys to a plate and keep warm. Add to the pan the crushed juniper berries and the spring onion and cook for 2 minutes. Now add the stock and reduce slightly over high heat. Remove the pan from the heat and add the cold butter cut up into small cubes. Swirl the pan around to incorporate the butter to make a sauce. Thinly slice the kidneys, season with a little salt and freshly ground black pepper and return to the pan together with the lemon juice. Stir quickly to re-heat and serve, together with the pan juices, over cooked rice.

FRENCH VERSION OF GNOCCHI
Serves 6

Other countries' versions of these light dumplings are made from semolina, potatoes or ricotta cheese. These little beauties are very light in texture and as well as beginning a meal can also be used in other ways: with a fresh tomato sauce lightly poured over them; as an addition to chicken soup; or used in place of potatoes with a lightly sautéed meat dish. Here we coat them with a cream sauce flavoured with cheese but if you wish, you can cut out the sauce, coat them with a mixture of cheese and some grated Parmesan and grill them until brown.

> 1½ cups water
> 2 tablespoons butter
> ¼ teaspoon salt
> 1½ cups plain flour, sifted
> 3 large eggs
> 3 tablespoons tasty grated cheese, either Parmesan or Cheddar
> 1 teaspoon mustard powder
> Dash of cayenne pepper
> Freshly ground white pepper
> A heaped teaspoon of salt

These are very akin to making choux pastry but the quantities are slightly different. Although it is possible to make the mixture in a food processor when you are adding the eggs one at a time to the paste, we still prefer to beat them in one at a time by hand with a wooden spoon. Bring water, butter and salt to the boil in a large saucepan. Remove from heat, tip the saucepan slightly and then beat in the flour. When mixture is smooth, beat in the eggs one at a time until the mixture is smooth and shiny. It takes a bit of work, we can assure you. Mix in the cheese, mustard and a little cayenne pepper and white pepper. Add a heaped teaspoon of salt to a large saucepan of water and heat until simmering, not a rolling boil. Scoop up a rounded teaspoon of the paste and shape into a ball with wet hands. Place enough of these into the pan of simmering water to make a single layer, do not overcrowd. The reason for this is that they swell and could stick together. Poach gently for about 15–20 minutes, never letting the water come to a rolling boil. They automatically keep turning themselves over as the underneath portion swells and gets lighter, so generally there is no need to stand there all the time to supervise. After cooking each batch, carefully remove with a slotted spoon to drain and place in a buttered oven-proof dish. Cover with the Cream Sauce (see below), sprinkle some extra grated cheese on the top and grill until golden brown and heated through.

Cream Sauce

> $1\frac{1}{2}$ cups cream
> Dash of salt and cayenne
> 3 tablespoons grated cheese
> Extra grated cheese for grilling

Bring the ingredients to the boil, stirring all the time until the cheese has melted, and pour over the cooked gnocchi. Grill with some extra grated cheese sprinkled over the top. You can reduce the amount of cream sauce to suit your own taste.

FROSTED CHEESE MOULD
Serves 8–10

We usually use this to begin a light meal in the
warmer weather, but with the addition of some
frosted seedless white grapes, melon balls and
orange segments we also serve it to end a meal in
the cooler weather instead of the more traditional
cheese and fruit. We always set this in a ring mould
of about 6-cup capacity so that we can fill the centre
with fruit or fruits as suggested above. Served with
dry, lightly toasted brown bread or wholemeal
crackers, it goes a long way.

> $1\frac{1}{2}$ cups milk
> $1\frac{1}{2}$ tablespoons gelatin powder
> About 700 grams ($1\frac{1}{2}$ lb) cottage cheese
> About 100 grams (4 oz) blue cheese (in NZ we use
>   Blue Vein), crumbled
> 2 tablespoons fresh lime juice
> $\frac{1}{2}$ cup lightly salted cashew nuts, toasted and
>   chopped
> Few drops green food colouring
> 1 cup cream, lightly whipped

Pour the milk into a large saucepan and sprinkle
over the gelatin. Let it soften and then heat the
milk, stirring to distribute the gelatin. Heat gently
and stir until the gelatin has dissolved, then remove
from the heat and leave to cool. Sometimes it can
take on a slightly curdled appearance, but don't
worry. Beat the cottage cheese and blue cheese together until well blended and stir into the milk. This

still leaves a slightly lumpy texture, so if you want it very smooth you may mix the cheeses in a food processor until smooth; we don't but you might like to. Add the lime juice, nuts and just enough food colouring to tint it a pale green, and mix well. Fold in the whipped cream and pour into the lightly oiled ring mould. Chill for 4–6 hours. Dip the ring for a few seconds into hot water, and unmould on to a serving plate. Fill the centre with fruit if you wish, or with some mint leaves for decoration.

MUSHROOM CAKE
Serves 8–10

We prefer to serve this at the beginning of a meal, but it can be served in the middle, in which case it will serve fewer people. The reason for using button mushrooms is the fact that they do not turn the end result into a grey mush, which the large open mushrooms would do. If the darker colour doesn't faze you at all, use the same weight of larger mushrooms for they definitely give a stronger mushroom flavour.

> 2 tablespoons clarified butter
> 500 grams (18 oz) button mushrooms, sliced
> 250 grams (9 oz) finely sliced onions
> 300 grams (11 oz) cooked, peeled, potatoes
> 4 eggs
> 250 grams (9 oz) cottage cheese
> $\frac{1}{4}$ cup cream

Good pinch freshly grated nutmeg
A little salt to taste
A little parsley, finely chopped and a few extra
uncooked mushrooms, thinly sliced, for dec-
oration (optional)

Melt the butter in a large pan with a lid. Gently fry
the mushrooms and the onions with the lid on over
a low heat for about 15 minutes, stirring around
now and again to prevent sticking. The reason for
this is that you are using very little butter and therefore the vegetables start to sweat. Now continue
cooking with the lid off over a higher heat, again
stirring, to dry off that excess moisture as you want
the end result to be pretty dry. Cook the potatoes
until soft, drain and dry them out in the saucepan
so that there is no excess moisture. Place the onions,
mushrooms and potatoes into a large bowl and
mash together well. Do not place into a food processor as you will destroy the texture. Mash, however, until well combined and fairly smooth. Beat in
the eggs one at a time, then the cottage cheese and
lastly the cream. Season with nutmeg and some
salt. Mix all together to form a thick paste. Lightly
butter a high-sided ring tin, about 6 cups capacity,
and pour in the mixture. Bang the tin on a solid
surface to get rid of any air pockets and smooth
over the surface of the mixture to make it level.
Place in a baking dish and fill the baking dish with
hot water to come halfway up the side of the ring
tin. Bake in the centre of a pre-heated oven set at
Gas Mark 7 (425°F, 220°C) for 30 minutes. Remove
from the oven and leave to settle for about 10

minutes. Run a thin knife around the edges and the centre to loosen, remove from the water, and pat the outside of the tin dry. Place a large warm plate on the top of the ring, carefully invert to loosen the mushroom cake and then remove the ring tin. Decorate the top if you wish with the parsley and the extra mushrooms.

STUFFED SQUID
Serves 4

We have all had it deep fried, haven't we? Well, if you have never tried it, do so, as it is really very good. One thing to remember is that squid either cooks for seconds or about an hour; in between those times you usually end up with a rubbery experience. We suggest that you buy already cleaned squid sacks measuring about 5–6 inches in length. As this is a fairly substantial beginning to a meal, a light middle course to follow is a good idea.

> *4 medium-sized squid sacks*
> *Fresh breadcrumbs dried in the oven*
> *Virgin olive oil*

The Sauce

> *1 large onion, finely chopped*
> *2 tablespoons olive oil*
> *2 large bayleaves*
> *1 clove garlic, crushed*

Good tablespoon plain flour
$\frac{1}{3}$ cup dry vermouth
$\frac{1}{3}$ cup water
A little salt and black pepper

The Stuffing

1 large onion finely chopped
3 tablespoons olive oil
3 large tomatoes, skinned, seeded and chopped
2 thick slices of bread soaked in milk and squeezed
   dry
1 clove garlic, crushed
2 tablespoons finely chopped parsley
2 egg yolks
A little salt and black pepper

Start by making the sauce. Sauté the onion in the olive oil over moderate heat until soft, add the bayleaves, garlic and flour and stir to amalgamate. Now pour in the vermouth, water and a little salt and pepper. Stir together and when simmering, cover with a lid and simmer for 15 minutes. Remove from heat. When cool remove the bay leaves.

To make the stuffing, sauté the onion in a fairly large pan in the oil until soft, add the tomatoes and a little salt and pepper and continue to cook until the moisture has evaporated. Add the squeezed bread, garlic and parsley and mix well. Remove from the heat and mix in the beaten egg yolks. You may have to add a little water to turn this into a thick moist paste, but don't over moisten. Chill. Divide the mixture equally between the tubes; don't overfill because the mixture will expand. Secure both ends of the tubes with toothpicks to prevent the stuffing oozing out too much while being cooked. Lightly oil a baking dish just large enough to hold the squid in a single layer. Place them side by side in it and pour over the sauce. Sprinkle fairly thickly with the dried fresh breadcrumbs and drizzle over some oil. The crumbs must be thick enough to act as an insulation and protect the surface of the squid from drying out. Bake at Gas Mark 3 (325°F, 170°C) for about 50 minutes until the crumbs are golden and the squid are tender when you test them by inserting a skewer.

NOTE To make the crumbs, remove the crusts from several slices of thick bread and drop through the feed tube of a food processor while the motor is running. Don't process too fine. Spread on to a metal baking tray and bake for about 10 minutes at Gas Mark 4 (350°F, 180°C) or until dry but not browned. You need the crumbs to be fairly coarse.

SQUID PIE
Serves 6

We prefer to serve this as a beginning to a light meal rather than in large portions as a middle course. However you may wish to have it as a main course once you have tasted it, and all it really needs to accompany it is a lovely fresh mixed green salad. It's really like a double crusted pizza than a pie and is stunning, although really very simple. We suggest that you buy prepared cleaned squid sacks up to about 6 inches in length. You can be more traditional and use whole baby squid, tentacles and all, but we feel that the 'nervous' would rather take our advice and use the sacks. The pastry is a little different and contains olive oil. We strongly suggest you buy the best oil, such as virgin oil. Start with the filling, and while it is cooling down make the pastry, which does require several 'rest periods' for it to be successful.

Filling

> 500 grams (18 oz) cleaned prepared squid
> 2 large bayleaves
> 2 large onions, finely chopped
> 3 tablespoons good olive oil
> 4 large tomatoes, skinned, seeded and chopped
> 1 large red pepper, seeded and chopped

Pastry

> 2 large eggs
> ½ teaspoon salt
> ¼ cup milk
> ¼ cup good olive oil
> 1 tablespoon melted lard
> Approx. 3 cups plain flour

Start by simmering the squid and the bayleaves in plenty of plain water in a saucepan with a tight-fitting lid, to stop the squid becoming dry, for 30 minutes. Drain, and when cool enough to handle, chop the squid into small pieces. In a medium-sized stainless or enamel saucepan sauté the onions in the oil over moderate heat until soft, then add the tomatoes, red pepper and the cut-up squid. Simmer together gently for 15 minutes and season to taste. Leave to cool while you make the pastry.

Mix together the eggs, salt, milk, olive oil and the melted lard in a large mixing bowl. Stir in the flour gradually until you have added sufficient to make a moist dough that will not stick to your fingers when kneaded together. Knead into a ball and leave covered for 15 minutes in a cool place. Press out on to a floured dinner plate and leave covered again for another 15 minutes. Divide the dough in half and roll half out into a round about 12 inches across. Place carefully on a lightly oiled baking tray. Spoon the cooled filling on to the pastry and distribute over it to within 1 inch of the edge. Roll the remaining dough into a circle slightly smaller than the first. Brush the edges of the bottom crust with cold water and place the smaller circle on top of the filling. Press the edges together all round to seal and then turn the edges of the bottom dough over the top to make it even more secure. Prick the top in several places with the prongs of a fork and bake at Gas Mark 4 (350°F, 180°C) in the centre of the oven until golden brown, about 30 minutes. Remove and leave to settle for 10 minutes and then carefully slip on to a large serving plate or board. Cut into wedges to serve.

DOUBLE FRIED CHICKEN WINGS WITH SICHUAN PEPPER
Serves 6 or more

These are terribly simple to do and can be used as
nibbles or as part of a Chinese meal. They are best
started a day before you want to cook them to allow
the marinade to penetrate and give them flavour.
The Sichuan peppercorns can be purchased at any
oriental food store and do make a difference to the
end result. They look like white peppercorns but in
fact they do have a different flavour.

> *Approx. 1 kilo (2¼ lb) chicken wings*
> *2 inch piece of fresh green ginger*
> *4–6 large cloves garlic*
> *2 tablespoons dark soy sauce*
> *4 tablespoons whisky or bourbon*
> *Cornflour for dusting*
> *2 cups either peanut or vegetable oil*
> *1 tablespoon Sichuan peppercorns*
> *1 tablespoon salt (not iodized)*

Cut the ginger into about three slices and crush
with the blade of a large knife or cleaver and put in
a fairly large bowl. Crush the unpeeled garlic cloves
in the same way and add to the bowl, together with
the soy and the whisky or bourbon. With a pair of
kitchen scissors cut off the tips of the wings and
reserve to make some stock at a later time. Twist
the remaining part of the wing at the central ball
joint and cut through with the scissors so that you
have two small pieces of wing. Put these into the

marinade and toss well with a large spoon to coat. Cover the bowl and place in the fridge, tossing the wings around in the marinade often, for at least 12 hours. When you are ready to serve, remove the wings from the marinade and place on paper towels to drain. Liberally dust them on both sides with cornflour and place on a wire rack to dry out. Heat the oil, preferably in a wok as it uses less, until it just starts to smoke. Fry the chicken in small batches until light golden brown, remove with a slotted spoon and keep to one side until all have been fried once. Return them, again in small batches, to the oil and re-fry until dark golden brown and crisp. Drain on kitchen paper and put into a heated bowl. Serve with the Sichuan pepper mixture in a separate bowl so that guests can dip them in when eating.

To prepare the pepper mixture, simply heat the peppercorns and salt in a small dry frying-pan for about 2 minutes over fairly high heat. Remove and grind together to form a powder. You can do this in a small grinder, such as a coffee grinder – which we keep for doing only spices and making curry powders, Garam Masala etc. – or in a pestle and mortar or through a pepper grinder. The amount will serve at least six as a nibble or beginning course and more if used as part of a Chinese meal.

Middles

CRISP FRIED FISH WITH LEMON SAUCE
Serves 4–6

If you are going to have fried fish in batter then you might as well do it right. This recipe we devised when we had our own Fish and Oyster Restaurant several years ago. The dish was extremely popular and when we eventually tried to take it off the menu and offer some alternative there were violent complaints from our many regular customers. We also used to serve with it this delicious lemon sauce which has a tendency to cut down the richness. The batter can be made a little while in advance, but the egg whites must only be beaten and added just prior to cooking the fish. Two other points are that you must have really fresh fish fillets and also clean clear oil for deep frying. We use either a combination of safflower and peanut oil or all peanut, and we also prefer to deep fry small amounts of the battered fish in a wok rather than a deep fryer as it uses less oil. If you have to keep the fried fish warm before serving, do so in a dish lined with crumpled paper towels in a low oven, but leave the door ajar slightly so that the steam doesn't collect and turn the batter soggy.

1 kilo ($2\frac{1}{4}$ lb) of firm fish fillets
Plain flour for dusting
Peanut oil for deep frying
6 spring onions

Batter

> 1 cup plain flour
> Pinch salt
> 1 tablespoon peanut oil
> 1 cup water, approx.
> 2 egg whites

Lemon Sauce

> 2 cups chicken stock
> 2 large strips of lemon peel
> $\frac{2}{3}$ cup of lemon juice
> Good 2 inch piece of fresh green ginger, sliced
>   thinly
> $\frac{1}{3}$ cup tightly packed soft brown sugar
> 2 tablespoons arrowroot mixed with a cup of
>   water

Cut the fillets into fingers and coat lightly in the flour. Dip in the batter and drain off the excess. Heat the oil in a large pan or wok and lower several pieces of the coated fish into the hot oil. Fry until light golden brown, which only takes a few minutes. Don't be tempted to overcrowd the cooking pot or wok. Drain each batch on kitchen paper and keep warm until you have cooked all the fish. Place on a heated serving dish, chop up the spring onions and sprinkle on the top. Finally pour over the lemon sauce, and try and serve it before it goes soggy. If you wish you can serve the sauce separately.

For the batter, sift the four and salt into a medium-sized bowl and add oil and enough water to make a fairly thick batter. Beat well and leave to stand for at least 20 minutes. Just before using, beat the egg whites until fairly stiff and fold into the batter.

The sauce is made by putting the chicken stock, lemon rind and juice into a heavy-based medium-sized pot, adding the sliced ginger and sugar. Bring to the boil, lower the heat, covering and gently simmering for 10 minutes. Strain the sauce to get rid of solids and pour back into the saucepan. Add the arrowroot mixed with water to the sauce. Stir until the sauce comes back to the boil and thickens. Simmer one minute more and serve.

NOTE It is fairly acceptable to use 2 cups of water and either a chicken stock cube or a teaspoon of chicken stock powder instead of the chicken stock if you have no home-made stock available. Check the seasoning when the sauce is finished. This sauce is also very good served over warm poached salmon steaks or other types of plain poached fish.

WHOLE FRIED FISH WITH GINGER SAUCE
Serves 2–4

Although this dish can be used as part of a Chinese meal when you have a large guest list, it is rather nice to serve either 2–4 people when you want something light and tasty as your middle course. There is always the question of what fish to buy. The type is a purely personal choice, but it really has to be a firm fleshed fish of the non-oily variety. It must be extremely fresh, and also must be gutted, scaled and the fins trimmed off. We cook ours whole with the head on, but you can remove the head if you like, especially if the whole thing would be too big for your wok. You can cook this in a large shallow frying-pan but we generally prefer a wok as it actually needs less oil.

> 1 whole fish, about 1 kilo (2¼ lb)
> Seasoned flour
> Peanut oil for frying
> 8 dried Chinese mushrooms
> 6 tablespoons white vinegar
> 6 tablespoons raw sugar
> ¾ cup water
> 2 tablespoons dark soy sauce
> 2 tablespoons finely chopped spring onions
> 1 tablespoon arrowroot
> 2 tablespoons water
> 4 tablespoons chopped fresh green ginger

Rinse the prepared fish thoroughly inside and out and pat dry with paper towels. Using a sharp cleaver or knife, score the fish deeply, almost to the bone, in lines cross-crossing to form a diamond pattern on both sides. The cuts should be about 1½ inches apart. Rub the seasoned flour on both sides, making sure it enters the cuts. Heat the oil, if using a shallow pan, to the depth of about 1 inch. Do this in either a shallow pan or, as we have mentioned earlier, a wok, in which case pour into the wok about 1 cup of oil. Fry very carefully on both sides until brown and crisp in the hot oil. Drain on crumpled kitchen paper and transfer to a heated serving dish. Pour the hot sauce over and serve straight away.

The sauce can be made several hours ahead, without the ginger being added until the re-heating stage. To do this, first soak the Chinese mushrooms in hot water for about 20 minutes. Remove the tough stalks and slice the caps across thinly. Reserve the water if you wish, and use in the quantities described to finish off the sauce. Place the sliced mushroom caps into a saucepan together with the vinegar, sugar, water, soy sauce and spring onions and boil, stirring occasionally for 5 minutes. Mix the arrowroot and 2 tablespoons of water together and add to the sauce. Cook until thickened, stirring to prevent lumps. Add the chopped green ginger at the re-heating stage prior to serving, or just at the end of cooking if it is to be used at once. Stir and pour over the fish.

FISH FILLETS WITH MUSHROOM STUFFING
Serves 4

We suggest smallish thin fillets, such as sole or flounder, for this particular recipe. You should really have the fillets skinned and boned, but we have occasionally cooked the dish with the skin still attached. If you cannot get your supplier to skin them for you, it really isn't too difficult to do it yourself. You will need a long sharp thin knife and

a solid board on which to perform the operation.
Lay the fillet skin side down and cut about an inch
away from the end at the tail end. Pressing your
fingers on the skin, place the knife at a shallow
angle and with a slight sawing motion cut away the
flesh from the skin. Do this while pressing the knife
blade downwards towards the skin. Take your time
and you will end up with a lovely skinless fillet. Use
the skins and a few heads to make some fish stock.

> 8 skinned fillets
> 2 tablespoons of brandy or cognac
> 4 large mushrooms, finely chopped
> 2 spring onions, finely chopped
> 2 thick slices bread, crusts removed and turned
>   into crumbs
> 2 tablespoons finely chopped parsley
> 1 teaspoon lemon juice
> A little salt and freshly ground black pepper
> $\frac{1}{2}$ cup dry white wine or dry vermouth
> $\frac{1}{2}$ cup water

In a glass or ceramic dish lay out four of the fillets
and sprinkle with one tablespoon of the brandy or
cognac. Lay the other four fillets on top of the first
four and again sprinkle with the rest of the spirit.
Cover and chill while you make the filling. The
mushrooms and spring onions can be chopped in a
food processor; also it can be used to turn the bread
into crumbs – no need to wash between each operation. Mix together the mushrooms, onions, breadcrumbs, parsley, lemon juice and a little salt and
pepper in a large bowl. The mixture should just

hold together; if it is a little too dry then add a touch of water to bind, but do not make it too wet. Butter an ovenproof dish that is large enough to hold four of the fillets in a single layer without overlapping. Divide the mushroom mixture equally between them and spread over each fillet with a knife. Place the other four fillets on top. Press down lightly and dot with a little butter. Pour around them the wine and water, plus any liquid that was in the marinading dish. Cover with buttered foil and bake at Gas Mark 4 (350°F, 180°C) for 25 minutes. Remove the fillet 'sandwiches' carefully to warm plate with a slotted fish slice, cover with the foil and keep warm while you make the sauce.

The Sauce

> Poaching liquid from the cooked fish
> 2 level teaspoons cornflour
> $\frac{3}{4}$ cup cream
> 1 teaspoon Dijon mustard
> Extra lemon juice to taste

Put the poaching liquid in a shallow frying-pan and boil until reduced to about a quarter cup. Mix the cornflour and cream and add to the pan. Whisk together until the mixture boils, lower the heat and whisk in the mustard. Transfer the fish 'sandwiches' to four warm serving plates and tip any juices into the sauce. Check the sauce for seasoning and sharpen with a little lemon juice. Spoon the sauce over the fillets and serve immediately with buttered julienne of carrots, leeks, courgettes that have been steamed until just cooked but still remain crisp to the bite.

SCALLOP AND SNAPPER MOUSSE
Serves 6

This is a very delicious way of stretching the flavour of scallops. Instead of snapper you may use any white, firm-fleshed, non-oily fish fillets. To really make it a dish fit for an Emperor, serve a lobster sauce to go with it. In actual fact we cheat and use a tin of either scampi or lobster bisque, heat it through in a small saucepan and then add a little cream and lastly, just before serving hot, a squeeze of lemon juice just to zip it up a bit. No one seems to notice, and they think that you have slaved away making it by boiling lobster shells and straining them etc., which you can do if you have the time. If you decide not to serve a sauce with it, it still holds its own very well served straight with lemon wedges. If you should find it too rich as a middle course, then you can serve it as a beginning course, in which case it will serve twice the number.

> *500 grams (18 oz) of snapper or similar fillets*
> *250 grams (9 oz) scallops, frozen are acceptable in this instance*
> *2 eggs*
> *3 extra egg whites*
> *Salt, white pepper, tabasco and grated nutmeg to taste*

1 tablespoon of tomato paste
600 millilitres (1 pint) cream
Butter for greasing

Check the fillets to see that there are no small bones or scales and cut into small pieces. Place them into a food processor fitted with the steel blade, and process until pulpy. You may have to stop the machine once or twice and scrape the sides of the bowl. Add a pinch each of salt, pepper and nutmeg, plus one whole egg and two of the whites. Continue to process until you end up with a smooth paste. Then gradually pour 400 ml (⅔ pint) of cream through the feed tube while the motor is running until you have a thick fish cream. Remove from the bowl with a spatula and place into a glass bowl, cover and chill.

Remove any sand tracks from the scallops and place into the processor. You don't have to rinse the bowl out. Add a little salt, pepper, nutmeg and tabasco and process until smooth. Add the second whole egg and the remaining egg white plus the tomato paste (this is only to enhance the colour) and process for 30 seconds. Pour the remaining cream through the feed tube while the motor is running. Again you will end up with a scallop cream, but much thinner than the fish one. Scrape into another small glass bowl, cover and chill. Leave both these mixtures to chill for about 1 hour.

Heavily butter a terrine or loaf tin, and spoon in half the fish cream then pour on the scallop cream. Rap the terrine or tin on the work bench to expel any air bubbles (not too hard or the scallop mixture might slop over you). Carefully spoon on the remainder of the fish cream and cover with a well-buttered double thickness of foil. Place the terrine in a larger ovenproof dish and fill the dish with hot water to come halfway up the terrine. Bake at Gas Mark 4 (350°F, 180°C) for 50 minutes. Remove from the oven and leave to stand in the hot water bath for 15 minutes or up to 30 minutes before serving. Carefully remove the foil and run a thin knife around the edges of the mousse to loosen. Place a warm serving plate on top of the terrine and with the aid of oven gloves to stop you getting burnt, invert the whole thing quickly. Wiggle the terrine to loosen completely. Cut into thickish slices and serve on warm serving plates together with either the lemon wedges or the lobster sauce (wink, wink) as described at the beginning. Serve any vegetable that you decide upon on separate plates.

If you want to serve it as a beginning to a meal it will serve 10–12 people. The portions won't look terribly large, but it is quite rich and very filling.

SCALLOP MOUSSE WITH SMOKED SALMON AND SAUTÉED CUCUMBER
Serves 4

We deviate here by including a vegetable with the main event. As a middle course this is rather rich but totally delectable. A simple crisp salad and bread and cheese, and perhaps a stunningly ripe peach or pear to end is all that you require for a sumptuous meal. We generally have our eye to cost in most of our dishes that we present, but on the odd occasion we let our heads go and have something a little over budget. So go on, treat yourself. You will need several slices of smoked salmon, enough for four persons, to lay as a base for each mousse. The recipe is set out with ingredients for the mousses, the sauce, the sautéed cucumber and we also include a simple fish stock because you need it for the sauce.

The Mousse

> 375 grams (13 oz) scallops (if fresh are un-available use frozen)
> 1 large egg
> Few grindings fresh nutmeg
> 1 teaspoon tomato paste
> Salt and white pepper (optional)
> 1 cup cream
> Butter for greasing
> Smoked salmon slices (at least 4) for base

The Sauce

> 3 cups strained fish stock
> $\frac{1}{2}$ cup dry vermouth
> 2 spring onions, finely chopped
> $1\frac{1}{4}$ cups cream
> 2 teaspoons cornflour mixed with a little water
> 125 grams ($4\frac{1}{2}$ oz) cleaned scallops
> Squeeze of lemon juice (optional)

Sautéed Cucumber

>   1 long cucumber
>   25 grams (1 oz) unsalted butter

Simple Fish Stock

>   Bones, head and skin from approx. 3 flounder or
>   sole
>   3 slices of onion
>   4 sprigs parsley
> $\frac{1}{2}$ carrot and one stalk celery, thinly sliced
>   6 whole peppercorns
>   1 cup dry white wine or dry vermouth
>   2 slices lemon
> $3\frac{1}{2}$ cups water

Skip to, and make the fish stock first by putting everything into a large enamel or stainless saucepan. Bring gently to simmering point and simmer very gently for a maximum of 20 minutes uncovered, skimming off any scum that may rise to the surface. Strain through a muslin lined sieve and leave to cool. Easy.

Now we attack the mousses. If the scallops happen to be frozen leave to thaw gently in the fridge overnight. Rinse the scallops quickly under cold water, remove any sand tracks from them, and cut them into pieces. Put them in a food processor fitted with the metal blade and process until puréed. Add the egg, nutmeg and tomato paste (which enhances the colour) and, if you wish, a little salt and white pepper. Switch on the motor and gradually pour the cream through the feed tube. When you have poured in all the cream continue to process for a further 30 seconds. Transfer to a glass bowl, cover and pop in the fridge for 30 minutes to chill. Thoroughly butter the insides of four one-cup china moulds. Cut four squares of foil large enough to cover each mould and butter well. Divide the mixture equally between the four moulds, cover with the buttered foil and place in an ovenproof dish. Pour in enough hot water to come halfway up the moulds. Set the oven to Gas Mark 4 (350°F, 180°C) and bake in the centre for about 20–25 minutes or until just set. Remove from the oven and leave in the water while you finish off the sauce (see below). Then lay the smoked salmon on to four dinner plates, remove the mousses and run a thin knife around the edges to release them and turn out on to the salmon. Top the mousses with some of the sauce, place the sautéed cucumber (see below) to one side of each mousse and serve with the extra sauce in a separate sauce boat. If you wish you can serve slices of wholemeal bread or rolls to mop up the extra sauce . . . smashing!

Now for the first part of the sauce. While the mousse mixture is chilling, pour the strained fish stock into a large saucepan and boil until reduced to ½ cup of concentrate; tip into a bowl and leave to cool. Boil the vermouth and the spring onions together in a stainless steel saucepan until you have about 2 tablespoons of liquid left and tip through a sieve into the fish concentrate. While the mousses are cooking in the oven, place this fish and vermouth essence into another saucepan together with the cream and the cornflour and water mixture and bring to the boil while whisking to prevent any lumps. Lower the heat and simmer for 10–15 minutes, stirring occasionally. Slice the cleaned scallops thinly and add to the sauce and heat through for no longer than 3 minutes, otherwise they will toughen. Squeeze a little lemon juice into the sauce if you like a sharper taste and spoon some of the sauce over each cooked mousse and serve the rest in a separate warm sauce boat.

Lastly the cucumber. Cut the cucumber in half lengthwise and remove the seeds with a small spoon. Slice into ½inch thick pieces and put into a pot of lightly salted water for 20 seconds, drain and refresh under cold water and drain again. Heat the butter in a large frying-pan and sauté the cucumber slices until just heated through; you are not cooking them, just heating so that they remain crisp. Place beside the mousses on the bed of salmon.

There you are, not really difficult but certainly very scrumptious.

LAYERED FISH (TROUT) IN BRIOCHE
Serves 8–10

When we start talking about dishes that are layered, most people throw their hands up in horror. Believe us when we say that this dish is really worth the effort, particularly if you are in an entertaining mood, because it can be done a day in advance, and all you have to do then is roll out the brioche dough,

plonk on the layered filling, wrap it up and bake it –
very easy. You will notice that we have called this
layered fish with trout in brackets. The reason is
that it is ideal to use trout fillets as they go a long
way when served in this manner, but you can still
make the dish with a lesser flavoured fish as long as
you use the smoked roe. Thin fillets of salmon are
also wonderful to use and are more economical than
you would imagine as the dish serves a lot of people.
We use whipped lemon butter to accompany it, but
you can use just plain wedges of lemon if you want
to cut down on the calories.

> 1 recipe for brioche dough (see below)
> 1 or 2 small trout or 4 decent fish fillets
> 3 cups white wine fish stock (see below)
> 1 cup long grain rice
> 1 onion, finely chopped
> 375 grams (13 oz) butter (this includes enough if
>   you want to make lemon butter)
> 3 tablespoons cream
> 3 spring onions, finely chopped
> 500 grams (18 oz) mushrooms, thinly sliced
> 4 hard-boiled eggs, coarsely chopped
> 3 tablespoons smoked roe
> 1 egg, beaten
> Juice of 3 lemons
> Salt and white pepper to taste

We will take this section by section, starting with
the Brioche Dough as this has to be made one day
in advance of completing the finished dish.

Brioche Dough
Serves 8–10

> 1 packet dry yeast (1 tablespoon)
> $\frac{1}{4}$ cup warm water
> 1 tablespoon sugar
> $2\frac{1}{3}$ cups plain flour
> $\frac{1}{2}$ teaspoon salt
> 175 grams (6 oz) butter
> 3 eggs

Dissolve the yeast in the water together with the sugar and leave until it starts to effervesce. Sift the flour and salt into a large bowl and add the butter which has been slightly softened and cut up. Rub in by hand, or cut in with a pastry blender or two knives as though you were starting to make pastry, until you have the appearance of coarse bread-crumbs. You can do this in a food processor, but do not over mix as you need to keep the mixture at the crumb stage, not worked into a ball. Add the dissolved yeast to the flour and butter mixture in the mixing bowl and mix with a fork. Break the eggs into a small bowl and beat well together, then add to the flour mixture. Mix well with a fork, and place the resulting spongy mixture into a lightly floured clean bowl. Cover with clingwrap and leave to double in bulk in a warm place. If doing this in cold weather, the airing cupboard is a good place in which to leave it to rise. This can take anything from 1–2 hours. Punch down, cover again and leave in the fridge overnight until ready to use. When ready, lightly knead on a floured surface and roll out large enough to completely envelop the filling. Now this seems an odd way to make brioche, but this method works because here you are using it as a rolled out dough and not as you would usually use a brioche mixture. Let us now proceed to the next section which includes the stock, fish and rice.

Fish and Rice Segment

First make a very simple fish stock by using the following:

> About 250 grams (9 oz) fish trimmings (bones, small heads and some skin)
> 1 small onion, sliced
> 1 small carrot, sliced
> 4 sprigs parsley
> 1 bayleaf
> 8 whole peppercorns
> $2\frac{1}{2}$ cups water
> 1 cup dry white wine
> $\frac{1}{2}$ lemon

Put all the ingredients in an enamel or stainless steel saucepan and gently simmer uncovered for 20 minutes. Strain through a very fine sieve and use as directed.

Carefully poach the fish in the stock until just cooked, about 10 minutes for the trout and 5 for the fillets, remembering that they will be cooked again later. Remove from the stock, take off any skin and bone and put to one side. Strain and reserve the stock. Rinse the rice under running water until the water runs clear and then drain the rice. In a heavy-based saucepan with a tight-fitting lid melt 3 tablespoons of the butter and sauté the chopped onion until soft. Add the rice and continue cooking over moderate heat until the butter has been absorbed and the rice is lightly coloured. Season with a little salt and pepper, if desired, and pour in 2 cups of the reserved fish stock. Bring to the boil, cover and lower the heat and simmer very gently for 20 minutes until liquid has been absorbed, stirring once or twice. Stir in the 3 tablespoons of cream and leave on one side to cool.

Let us now move on to the mushroom segment.

Mushroom Segment

Melt a further 6 tablespoons of the butter in a large frying pan and sauté the chopped spring onions for 2 minutes. Add the sliced mushrooms and cook over fairly high heat for 5 minutes, stirring most of the time. Remove from heat and season, if desired, then leave to cool.

Assembling the Filling

Line a large loaf tin measuring 10 in × 5 in × 3 in with a double thickness of waxed paper. Alternatively, you can use two smaller tins and make two finished dishes instead of one large one. Now fill the tin or tins in layers in the following order:

a layer of rice
a layer of chopped hard-boiled eggs
a layer of mushrooms
a layer of smoked roe
a second layer of mushrooms
a second layer of chopped hard-boiled egg
a layer of the trout or fish fillets
a final layer of rice

Press down well, cover and chill in the fridge overnight. Turn out the filling on to the centre of the rolled out brioche dough; carefully remove any paper. Brush the edges of the dough with water and draw up to enclose the filling completely. Make sure that it is well sealed. It is best to assemble this on a baking tray that has been lightly buttered, otherwise it is difficult to manoeuvre the enveloped filling. Leave at room temperature for 30 minutes. Heat the oven to Gas Mark 5 (375°F, 190°C). When the oven is ready, brush the entire exposed surface of the dough with the beaten egg to glaze and bake in the middle of the oven for 20–30 minutes until golden brown. While this is baking, beat the lemon juice into the remaining softened butter for the sauce. Leave the cooked brioche to settle for 8 minutes when taken from the oven. Slice with a serated knife to serve. Stunning . . .

SMOKED FISH AND SQUID PIE
Serves 4

This is a good introduction to squid for people who
have never eaten it before. It extends the smoked
fish and is invariably cheaper than the former to
buy. Served together with its sauce, some tomatoes,
and topped with mashed potatoes and cheese, it is
very good indeed. We suggest serving also a green
vegetable or salad. Also for the squeamish, or for
that matter convenience, buy the squid sacks
already prepared and cut into about 5–6 inches in
length. Squid is cooked either very quickly or for a
long period to keep it tender. This recipe has an
advantage of being cooked in the liquid from the
fish which gives the squid more flavour.

> *1 piece of smoked fish, enough for 2 persons*
> *Water to cover*
> *2 squid sacks cut into strips*
> *25 grams (1 oz) butter*
> *1 medium onion, finely chopped*
> *1 tablespoon flour*
> *1 cup reserved stock (explained in recipe)*
> *¼ cup cream*
> *Salt and freshly ground black pepper*
> *3 large tomatoes, peeled and sliced*
> *About 4 medium-sized potatoes (enough when
>   mashed to cover filling)*
> *1 egg*
> *Extra cream and butter*
> *About ½ cup grated Cheddar cheese*

Cover the smoked fish with water and poach on top of the stove or in a microwave until tender. Remove the fish and reserve the stock. Flake the fish, making sure there are no bones or scales and keep to one side. Put the stock together with the squid strips in a saucepan, cover and simmer very gently for 30–40 minutes or until the squid is tender. Drain the squid, reserving one cup of the stock for the sauce. Cut the squid into small cubes and mix with the flaked fish. Melt the butter in a saucepan and add the onion. Cook gently until soft and lightly golden, about 6 minutes. Add the flour and stir together, then add the stock and bring to the boil, then add the cream. Lower the heat and simmer for a further 2 minutes, stirring to achieve a lump-free sauce. Remove from the heat and taste first, as it may be salty enough, before seasoning. Mix this sauce with the fish and squid and pour into a piedish. Cover with the slices of tomato. Peel and cook the potatoes until just tender, about 20 minutes, and mash together with some cream, beaten egg and butter plus seasoning. Don't make it too sloppy. Smooth the mashed potato over the filling and tomatoes in the dish and then cover with the grated cheese. Bake at Gas Mark 4 (350°F, 180°C) for about 20–30 minutes until the potatoes are golden brown.

SALMON AND RICE MOULD
Serves 6

In the warmer weather it is always nice to be able to prepare something in the cool of the morning to serve later. When you see a good brand of tinned salmon on special offer at your local store, buy up several tins for opportunities such as this. This is superb with a good salad of mixed types of salad greens and a lemony dressing to which you have added some fresh chopped dill.

> *450 grams (1 lb) tinned red salmon*
> *4 teaspoons gelatin powder*
> *2 cups well-flavoured chicken stock*
> *1 hard-boiled egg, sliced*
> *1 cup of cooked rice*
> *$\frac{1}{4}$ cup dry white wine*
> *A little salt and freshly ground white pepper to taste*
> *1 tablespoon chopped chives*
> *A few lettuce leaves*
> *Cucumber slices to garnish*

Most recipes tell you to remove the bones and skin from the salmon, but we have always found them so soft, that we just mash the whole lot together. Soften the gelatin in some cold water or cold chicken stock. Heat the chicken stock to almost boiling and add the softened gelatin. Stir until dissolved and leave to cool. Rinse a mould or loaf tin with cold water, drain and spoon in a layer of the cooled chicken stock, about $\frac{1}{4}$ inch deep, and leave in the fridge to set. When set, place the sliced egg on the jelly decoratively and spoon on some more chicken stock just to cover the egg and again put it into the fridge to set once more. Combine the remainder of the stock with the rest of the ingredients, with the exception of the lettuce leaves and cucumber, mix well and spoon into the prepared mould or tin. Leave to set for at least 4 hours. Dip in hot water to loosen, and turn on to a layer of lettuce leaves, decorate around it with cucumber slices. Serve as suggested above, but it is also nice to serve thin brown bread and butter.

TWO-WAY SPINACH ROULADE
Serves 4 and 6

The idea is that with the basic roulade mixture you can make it and serve it with a hot filling, in this instance mushrooms, or fill it when cold with a mixture of cream cheese and smoked salmon. The basic roulade, which after all is another version of a thin flat soufflé, is really very easy to do. We have found that when using fairly mature open mushrooms the end result can look a little on the grey or muddy side, so we prefer to use small closed button ones. Lots of people line their swiss-roll tin with buttered paper but again we have more control by using well-buttered foil instead.

For The Roulade

> 500 grams (18 oz) fresh spinach
> 1 tablespoon butter (and extra butter for greasing)
> A squeeze of lemon juice
> Freshly ground black pepper
> A few grindings of fresh nutmeg
> 4 large eggs, separated
> Freshly grated Parmesan cheese

Hot Mushroom Filling

> 225 grams (8 oz) button mushrooms, sliced
> 2 tablespoons butter
> 1 rounded tablespoon plain flour
> Seasoning to taste
> 1 cup milk
> ¼ cup cream

Cold Cream Cheese and Smoked Salmon Filling

> 1 cup of cream cheese
> 100 grams (4 oz) smoked salmon scraps
> Dash tabasco
> Juice of half a lemon, or to taste
> 1 spring onion, finely chopped
> ¼ of a red pepper, finely chopped

Line a swiss-roll tin with well-buttered foil, butter side up, making sure to turn the edges up about an inch all round. Wash the spinach and cook either in a saucepan, with only the water that clings to the leaves after they have been shaken, or in a microwave oven in a microwave-proof casserole. When cooked, squeeze as much water out of them as you can, either with your hands when it has cooled down or between two plates. Chop finely either by hand or in a food processor. Return the spinach back to a saucepan together with the butter, lemon juice, pepper and nutmeg. Stir over high heat to dry off excess moisture then remove from the stove top. Beat in the egg yolks one at a time. Whip the egg whites until stiff and gently but thoroughly cut them into the spinach mixture until well incorporated. Pour into the prepared butter foil and spread evenly. Dust with just enough Parmesan to cover the surface lightly and bake in a pre-heated oven Gas Mark 6 (400°F, 200°C) for 10 minutes or until well risen and firm to the touch.

While this is cooking prepare the mushroom filling. Quickly sauté the mushrooms in the butter over high heat for 2 minutes. Draw the pan aside and add the flour and seasoning, stir well and return to the heat. Add the milk and cook, stirring until you have a creamy sauce, then add the cream and again heat until bubbling. Remove the cooked roulade from the oven and turn out on to a large sheet of greaseproof paper. Carefully peel off the foil and spread half the mushroom filling on to the roulade to within about an inch all round, roll up like a swiss roll. Transfer to a heated serving dish and pour the remaining sauce along the top. This will serve four people, cut into 8 slices.

To proceed with the second way, first make the roulade and when cooked remove from the oven. Turn on to a large sheet of greaseproof paper that has been dusted with some extra Parmesan. Remove the foil carefully and roll up with the aid of the greaseproof paper, and when rolled leave to cool. Carefully unroll and spread the softened filling, directions for which are given below. Roll up the roulade again and wrap in some foil or clingwrap and chill slightly prior to serving, cut up into slices. This will feed six people as it is fairly rich.

To make the cold filling for this one, just soften the cream cheese, a microwave is ideal for this. Beat until soft and pliable in a bowl. Finely chop the smoked salmon scraps and mix in with the cheese together with the tabasco, lemon juice, spring onion and red pepper, or the mixture can be puréed in a food processor. When very pliable, carefully spread over the cooled roulade as described above, going almost to the edges and roll up again.

NOTE If you think that smoked salmon is too expensive you can use cooked well-flavoured smoked fish or smoked trout, providing that they are puréed or chopped finely before adding them to the cream cheese.

VEGETABLE TERRINE WITH HERB DRESSING
Serves 6

This makes a very satisfying meal in the warmer weather and can also be used at the beginning of a meal to serve a larger number of people. Should you feel the need to serve something with it, we suggest small steamed new potatoes coated with a little melted butter and freshly ground black pepper, but presented on a separate side plate. A fairly large long loaf tin or terrine is best used for this, and we have found from experience that when you are layering in the leeks, do so across the terrine and not lengthwise, the reason being that the leeks do not cut through very easily and have a tendency to 'pull out' when you are cutting the finished terrine into slices. The beans and carrots do not present this problem and therefore can be layered lengthwise. Good home-made chicken stock, de-fatted, is essential.

> 500 grams (18 oz) small leeks
> 500 grams (18 oz) medium-sized carrots
> 500 grams (18 oz) young green beans
> 500 grams (18 oz) young spinach
> 4 cups well-flavoured chicken stock
> ½ cup dry white wine
> 2 rounded tablespoons gelatin
> Seasoning to taste
> 4 spring onions, including green, finely chopped

Wash and trim the leeks of most of the green end and cut into lengths to fit the width of the tin or terrine (see above), then cut them lengthwise into julienne strips. Peel or scrub the carrots and also cut into julienne strips. Steam each separately until tender, about 10–12 minutes, drain and place on kitchen paper to dry. Chill. Trim and string the beans, cut in half and steam also until just tender, drain and also place on to kitchen paper. Chill. You may like to refresh each batch of vegetables in cold water to stop the cooking process and then drain and dry, before you chill them. Remove the stems from the spinach, rinse and cook by either steaming in a saucepan or microwave until just tender. Drain thoroughly. Squeeze dry and chop, then chill. Soften the gelatin in the wine while heating the clarified chicken stock. When the stock has almost reached simmering point add the softened gelatin and wine and stir until dissolved. Leave to cool and then chill until syrupy.

NOTE The next part tends to put people off. A lot of patience is involved in layering the stock and vegetables and waiting for each layer to set before proceeding. We know it takes a little effort and time, but you will be very proud when you eventually turn it out and see layers of vegetables suspended in clear crystal jelly.

Place about ½ cup of the cooled stock into the base of the tin or terrine, pop into the fridge to set. Arrange half the carrots, leeks and beans over this set layer and pour over enough stock to just cover. Back into the fridge to set once more. Spread over the chopped spinach, and sprinkle evenly with the chopped spring onion. Layer the remaining vegetable as before and again pour over the remainder of the stock. Cover the tin with foil or place the lid on the terrine. Back into the fridge to set for at least 5 hours or overnight.

Before serving you can put together the dressing

either by whisking everything together by hand or mixing it in a food processor or blender.

Herb Dressing

> $\frac{1}{4}$ cup tarragon vinegar
> 2 tablespoons water
> $\frac{1}{2}$ teaspoon each dried chervil, tarragon and salt
> $\frac{1}{4}$ teaspoon each dry mustard powder and black pepper
> $\frac{3}{4}$ cup of virgin oil or vegetable oil
> $\frac{1}{4}$ cup peanut oil
> 4 tablespoons finely chopped parsley
> 2 tablespoons chopped chives

As we have mentioned above, either whisk everything by hand until it emulsifies, or place the first seven ingredients into a food processor or blender, switch the motor on and drizzle the oils through the top so that the mixture emulsifies. Pour into a bowl and stir in the parsley and chives.

To serve, dip the terrine into hot water for only a few seconds and invert on to a large cold plate. Shake to release the jelly and then cut into thickish slices and serve on separate plates lined with lettuce. Pass the dressing separately.

LAYERED OMELET
Serves 8–12

At the very outset we want to explain that this dish takes some time to prepare. It seems a lot of trouble but we can assure you that the end result is worth the effort. As it will serve between 8–12 people it is relatively economical. It contains no meat but an awful lot of eggs, therefore containing plenty of protein. It is best made on the same day as you plan to serve it because it does not store at all well if you place it in the fridge. However, because it should only be served warm or at room temperature and not hot, once it has been cooked you can leave it to sit for several hours in the hot water bath and then turn it out and serve when you are ready.

> *425 grams (15 oz) fresh spinach*
> *3 tablespoons butter*
> *Good pinch fresh nutmeg*
> *Salt or squeeze of lemon juice*
> *Freshly ground black pepper*
> *3 tablespoons butter*
> *225 grams (8 oz) mushrooms, cleaned and thinly sliced*
> *1 tablespoon madeira*
> *Juice of half a lemon*
> *3 tablespoons butter*
> *1 cup finely chopped onion*
> *2 green peppers, seeded and finely chopped*
> *3 large ripe tomatoes, peeled, seeded and chopped*
> *2 teaspoons tomato paste*
> *1 teaspoon dried sweet basil or 1 tablespoon chopped fresh basil*

1 *tablespoon butter*
24 *eggs*
$\frac{1}{4}$ *cup cream*

Take your time and do this step by step as described hereafter. Take off the stalks of the spinach and wash it. With only the water that clings to it after it has been drained, cook either in a covered saucepan or on full power in a microwave until limp. Cool, squeeze as much liquid from it as you can, either between two plates or with your hands, and then chop it fairly finely. In a large heavy frying-pan, melt the first 3 tablespoons of butter, add the spinach, some grated nutmeg and a little salt and pepper or just pepper and a squeeze of lemon juice. Stir over fairly high heat until all moisture has evaporated. Remove from the pan and leave to cool on a plate. In the same pan (why bother to dirty another?) melt the next 3 tablespoons of butter and add the mushrooms. Cook for a few minutes, stirring all the time and add some pepper, madeira and lemon juice. Turn out of the pan once again after all the liquid has evaporated and add to the spinach. When both the spinach and mushrooms are cold, mix together in a bowl, easier than trying to do it on a plate. Wipe out the pan with some kitchen paper and then melt the third 3 tablespoons of butter and cook the onions and green peppers until slightly golden. Now add the tomatoes, tomato paste and basil and a little salt and pepper if desired. Stir-cook over a moderate heat until all the liquid has once again evaporated, and transfer to a separate bowl and leave to cool.

Take the 24 eggs and break them into a large bowl. To be on the safe side, break each egg separately into a cup first to check that it is a good one; it would be a disaster if you broke them straight into a large bowl and 23 were good and the last one was bad and tainted the whole lot. Beat them together and season, and divide the egg mixture into five equal amounts into five small bowls. Let's hope you have a dishwasher ... Wipe out your frying-pan again and tip one of the small bowls of beaten egg into it. Cook very gently until you obtain softly scrambled egg. Do not overcook as they will turn watery. Undercooking is better as they are going to be cooked again later on. Place on a separate plate and leave to cool. Go through this same procedure with three more bowls of egg placing each lot on a separate plate when cooked. Beat the cream into the remaining bowl of beaten egg. Butter a large loaf pan (12 in × 4¼ in × 3 in) or use two smaller ones. Line the bottom and sides with waxed paper and again butter the paper. Pour one third of the cream and egg mixture into the lined pan and spread on one batch of the scrambled egg over the top (do it gently). Spread half the tomato mixture over this and another batch of scrambled egg. Add all the spinach mixture to make one layer and cover this with another layer of scrambled egg. Don't give in; we are nearly there. Spread the remaining tomato mixture over the egg and top with the final batch of scrambled egg. Pour the remaining liquid egg and cream mixture carefully over the top and tap the tin carefully so that it seeps through the layers. Place the loaf tin into a baking dish and pour in enough hot water to come half way up the side of the loaf tin. Pre-heat the oven to Gas Mark 5 (375°F, 190°C). And just before you place it in the oven loosely cover the top of the layered omelet with a sheet of buttered foil, buttered side down. Cook in the centre of the oven for 40 minutes or until well puffed and just set. Try not to overcook, otherwise it will be too firm when served. Remove from the oven and let stand for at least 30 minutes. Take off the foil and carefully turn out on to a large serving dish by placing the plate upside down on top of the loaf tin. Quickly invert the whole thing. Carefully remove the tin and peel off the waxed paper. Cut into slices and serve, accompanied by a crisp green or mixed salad and some wholemeal rolls.

GLAZED CORNED (SALTED) SILVERSIDE
Serves 6

This is something many people overlook, yet a piece of perfectly cooked salted silverside is very hard to beat for flavour either hot or cold. It is ideal when serving a large group of people, but it can be used for a smaller number, leaving plenty for salads or sandwiches afterwards. Cooked this way and finished with the glaze, it takes on a different taste. The glaze may sound odd because of the ingredients used. A dear friend of ours, Beverly, gave this recipe to us years ago and it brings back fond memories of the meals we used to have with her.

2–2½ kilos (4½–5½ lb) piece of good corned silverside
(salted)
1 large carrot, sliced
1 large onion, quartered
3 sprigs parsley
2 stalks celery, thickly sliced
10 peppercorns
4 whole cloves
2 bayleaves
2 cloves garlic, peeled
2 tablespoons raw sugar
1 tablespoon vinegar

For the Glaze

1 small tin crushed pineapple
¼ cup chopped glacé cherries
½ cup bitter marmalade
4 tablespoons Dijon mustard
4 whole cloves

Put the piece of silverside in a large pot and add all
the first set of ingredients. Cover with cold water
and bring to boiling point, lower the heat, cover
and simmer very gently for between 2–2½ hours,
or until tender when tested with a skewer. When
cooked, remove from the pot, allow the liquid to
cool and replace the meat in it. We always like to
keep the meat in the cooking liquid to prevent it
drying out. We also prefer to slightly undercook the
meat rather than overcook, because it can become
very stringy. If in doubt about whether it has
cooked, remove it carefully from the simmering

liquid to a board and carve off a thin slice. If it is not to your liking, then return to the pot and cook a little longer.

To make the glaze just put the ingredients into a small heavy-based saucepan and bring gently to the boil, remove from the heat and stir well. Pre-heat the oven to Gas Mark 4 (350°F, 180°C). Line a baking dish with a double thickness of foil – this saves burnt glaze spoiling it – and place the drained meat in the centre. Cover with the glaze and bake for 20 minutes, spooning it frequently over the meat, until the glaze starts to turn a golden brown. Carefully remove to a carving dish and slice and serve straight away. We usually serve either plain boiled or mashed potatoes and steamed cabbage wedges. Scrumptious!

BARBECUED PORK SPARE RIBS
Serves 6

We want to mention several recipes for barbecueing as we do a lot not only in the summer but whenever the weather allows us to cook and eat outdoors. After trying for years to use charcoal as the heat source we succumbed to buying a gas-operated barbecue that is also fitted with a lid. It was quite an expensive outlay of cash but has really paid dividends over the years. A really good sturdy model will last for many, many years. The recipes that we give here can also be baked in the oven, but because they have basting sauces we strongly recommend that you line the baking dish with a heavy-duty double thickness of foil to prevent the dish getting ruined.

> 2 kilos (4½ lb) meaty pork spare ribs
> ¼ cup soft brown sugar
> 1 tablespoon salt
> 1 tablespoon celery seeds
> 2 teaspoons chilli powder
> 1 teaspoon paprika
> ¼ cup white vinegar
> 1 cup tomato sauce
> ¼ cup peanut oil

Mix all the dry ingredients together in a small bowl. Rub this mixture into the spare ribs well. Do this on a large sheet of waxed paper. Put the spare ribs to one side in a large dish, and tip any excess dry ingredients from the waxed paper back into the bowl. Pour the vinegar, tomato sauce and oil into the bowl of dry ingredients and mix well with a whisk. Now wash your hands . . . Heat the barbecue, low to medium heat, and cook the spare ribs, turning frequently, for about 15 minutes, then start basting them with the sauce. As this contains sugar, they can burn before they are fully cooked, so keep them a fair way from the heat source and turn and baste frequently for another 15–20 minutes until cooked. You can play safe by placing the ribs, once they have been rubbed with the dry ingredients, in a baking tray lined with foil and pre-cook them in the oven before barbecueing and basting with the sauce. Set the oven to Gas Mark 4 (350°F, 180°C) and cook for about 40 minutes, turning once halfway through. Then finish off on the barbecue, or if the weather turns inclement then continue in the oven, basting them with the sauce fairly frequently, also turning regularly until a dark mahogany colour and cooked through. The times given here are only estimates as a lot depends on the thickness and size and meatiness of the ribs.

This same mixture and method can be used for trimmed pork chops or even lamb chops; the cooking time, however, will be less in both cases. You can mix everything together to make a basting sauce and use it on the chops or chicken pieces, but we prefer to rub the dry mix well into the meat first and leave it for about an hour before proceeding to cook. They are hot in flavour and terribly more-ish.

BARBECUED CHICKEN PIECES
Serves 6

Make the sauce, which is uncooked, the day before to allow the flavours to mingle together. Several hours before cooking the chicken, slash the pieces several times on both sides and place in the sauce. Drain the chicken pieces before placing them on the barbecue over medium heat.

> $\frac{1}{2}$ cup dry cider
> $\frac{1}{4}$ cup peanut oil
> 2 teaspoons Worcestershire sauce

1 tablespoon finely chopped onion
2 cloves garlic, crushed
1 teaspoon salt
2 teaspoons paprika
1 tablespoon tomato paste
Dash of tabasco
3 tablespoons soft brown sugar
1 teaspoon dry mustard powder
1 inch piece of fresh green ginger, finely chopped
12 chicken pieces (we prefer legs or thighs)

Whisk all the sauce ingredients together in a glass bowl, then submerge the chicken pieces, turning them over to coat all their surfaces, and leave overnight. Drain the chicken pieces and cook gently for about 5 minutes, turning once. Then keep basting with the sauce, turning frequently until the chicken pieces are cooked and coloured a gorgeous brown. This will take about 15 minutes, depending on the thickness of the pieces used and the heat source. These can also be done in the oven in a tin lined with foil but heat the oven to Gas Mark 6 (400°F, 200°C) and cook for about 20 minutes in all.

MINTED BARBECUED LAMB SHANKS
Serves 4

These have to be started the day before. Because of their thickness, we prefer to cook them partially, prior to marinading, and then finish them off on a barbecue. So really what you are doing is giving them the flavour by marinading overnight and 'crusting' them and heating them through again on the barbecue. It is best to leave them out of the fridge for an hour or so at room temperature before cooking them on the barbecue. As with the Pork Spare Ribs these can be finally cooked in the oven if the weather turns foul.

> 4 medium-sized lamb shanks (*too big or old and they will be tough*)
> $\frac{3}{4}$ cup either dry white wine, sherry or madeira
> 2–3 tablespoons lemon juice
> 3 cloves garlic, crushed
> $\frac{1}{2}$ cup runny honey
> 4–6 tablespoons fresh mint, chopped
> 1 teaspoon salt and some freshly ground black pepper

Rinse the shanks and put into a large pot, just covering with cold water. Bring to the boil, and skim off any scum that rises to the surface. Lower the heat, cover and simmer very gently for about 45 minutes or until the shanks are just tender. This will depend on size and age, but please don't overcook so that they fall apart. Drain well. Now mix together all the other ingredients into a glass bowl or dish, not metal because of the wine, and place the warm shanks into the marinade. Leave to cool, turning them once or twice, cover and chill overnight. Baste them occasionally when you pass the fridge. Cook over moderate heat on the barbecue, turning and basting them frequently until nicely browned and tender.

CROWN ROAST OF LAMB
Serves 6

Although mentioned frequently in many books, there are certain points that we feel we should pass on to you. First, it is an ideal roast to bring and carve at table if you are an inexperienced carver, because all you have to do is cut down between the bones. Also it is not a good idea to fill the centre with some rice concoction or peas, as a lot of people do, because when you cut the chops, for that is what they are, apart all this middle stuff cascades down on to the carving plate which makes the dish difficult to serve. We have a small tin can that has been scrubbed and sterilised in the dishwasher which we use in the centre instead of a filling. This absorbs heat from the oven and helps the centre portion of the crown roast to cook; it also cooks the whole thing quicker. When we use this centre tin, we have a fairly high heat and allow a shorter cooking time so that the meat is still pink and moist when it is served. Any accompanying filling we cook separately and serve separately also. When you buy a crown roast ask for it to be prepared for you, for although it isn't too difficult to do oneself it helps take the time out of preparing the whole meal.

> 2 racks of lamb, trimmed and tied into a 'crown'
> 1 clove garlic, crushed
> ½ teaspoon salt
> ½ teaspoon powdered rosemary
> 3 tablespoons soft mustard (not hot English)
> 3 tablespoons peanut oil
> 1 teaspoon dark soy sauce
> 1 small tin can, both ends removed
> Kitchen foil

Stand the tied racks of lamb in a shallow baking tray. Mix together in a small bowl the garlic, salt, rosemary, mustard, oil and soy, and spread evenly over the outside of the meat to flavour it while it cooks. Place the tin can in the centre – it must be large enough to fit fairly tightly so that it touches the meat – and cover the bones with foil. You need to cover the chined bones because you are going to cook this at a high heat and if they are left uncovered there is a very strong chance that they will burn before the meat is cooked. Heat the oven to Gas Mark 9 (475°F, 240°C). Place the crown roast in the oven and cook for 10 minutes to sear the outside; lower the heat to Gas Mark 6 (400°F, 200°C) and cook for a further 15 minutes. Remove and keep warm and allow the juices to settle before carving. Remove the tin and the foil and place the roast on a serving plate to take to table and carve there. We like to serve it with simple things such as green beans or peas, new or plain boiled potatoes, minted of course, and small carrots.

NOTE This same 'cut' of meat can be cooked flat with the same baste spread over, but 15 minutes before the end take it from the oven and spread over a mixture of fresh breadcrumbs and some chopped parsley, both moistened with some melted butter and seasoned lightly. Then continue to bake for those last 15 minutes to get a nice crusty coating. Also we use the rack cut and cooked for Lemon Cutlets Piquant (page 82) and Cutlets in Pastry (page 84), both of which are ideal light middle courses and easy to do.

LEMON CUTLETS PIQUANT
Serves 4

These have the most delightfully sharp lemon flavour and are very easy to prepare and cook. Make sure that the excess fat has been trimmed off and that the bones have been chined. Depending on the size, three or four per person are enough. We suggest that small steamed potatoes are served with the cutlets on the plate and that a green vegetable is served on a small separate side plate. Having cooked this on numerous occasions over many years we have certainly increased the amounts of some of the ingredients since we first cooked it. We will quote the quantities that we like, but you might like to decrease them slightly for your first attempt. However, don't reduce the quantity of parsley.

12 lamb cutlets trimmed and chined
3 tablespoons clarified butter, or 1 butter and 2 oil
3 cloves garlic, finely chopped
2 tablespoons capers, chopped
6 tablespoons finely chopped parsley
Juice of 2 lemons

Flatten the meat end of the cutlets with either the flat side of a cleaver or a rolling pin. Heat the butter, or butter and oil, in a large, heavy-based frying-pan and add the garlic, capers and parsley. Stir around and evenly distribute over the base of the pan. Now fry the cutlets over a good heat, turning occasionally so that the cutlets are well coated with the mixture. Only cook for about a total of 5 minutes to ensure that they remain pink. When cooked, put them on a heated serving dish and keep hot. Add the lemon juice to the pan, mix well, bring to the boil and pour over the cutlets.

NOTE   You really do need a large pan to cook 12 cutlets together. If you haven't one, but do have a pan that will hold 6 of the cutlets at a time, then divide the butter, garlic, capers and parsley in half and cook two separate lots.

CUTLETS IN PASTRY
Serves 4 or 8

Cutlets are very useful, and done this way the cost
is extremely reasonable as we suggest only one per
person if served with vegetables, or two if you are
only serving a salad. We have done other stuffings
in other books but this one is really a little different.
We use tinned artichoke hearts as part of the stuffing. If the tin you buy contains more than you
need for this recipe use the rest another day sliced
up into a green salad with a lemony dressing. As
the filling is loose and not bound together with
anything, just pile on the top of each cutlet once
you have placed them on the pastry.

> 8 trimmed and chined lamb cutlets
> 1 tablespoon peanut oil
> 8 artichoke hearts, sliced
> 8 closed mushrooms, thinly sliced
> 1 tablespoon finely chopped parsley
> 2 spring onions, finely chopped
> A little salt and freshly ground black pepper
> Juice of half a lemon
> 4 pre-rolled pastry squares (fairly large ones
>   bought in a packet)

Flatten the trimmed cutlets with the side of a cleaver
or a rolling-pin and sear very quickly in the hot
peanut oil over high heat in a heavy-based frying-
pan. Place to one side to go cold. You don't want to
overcook them as they will be baked again later; all
you are doing is sealing in the juices. Mix together

in a medium-sized bowl the artichoke hearts, mushrooms, parsley, spring onions, salt and pepper and lemon juice. Cut the pastry sheets in half diagonally to make 8 large triangles. Place a cold cutlet on each triangle of pastry and divide the filling equally on top of each one. Moisten the edges of the pastry with water and wrap around each cutlet and filling to enclose, sealing well. Pre-heat the oven to Gas Mark 6 (400°F, 200°C). Butter or lightly oil a large baking sheet or tray and arrange the pastry parcels on it. Glaze each one with a little beaten egg and water or cream. Bake in the middle of the oven for 20 minutes or until nicely browned.

LAMB CHOPS PAPRIKA
Serves 4

For this dish it is best to use a casserole that can go from stove top to oven and then to table. You can leave the chops whole, but we generally like to cut them up into large chunks, which makes them easier to eat. Served with either plain steamed or mashed potatoes, it is a wonderfully comforting dish. We serve a green vegetable but on a side plate so that the sauce from the casserole doesn't drizzle into it. It also benefits the flavour to be made in advance prior to thickening, adding the yoghurt, tomatoes etc. as it gives the flavours a chance to amalgamate together.

8 mid loin chops, trimmed of excess fat and skin

1 tablespoon clarified butter
2 large onions, sliced
2 tablespoons fresh paprika
2 cloves garlic, crushed
2 tablespoons tomato paste
A little salt and black pepper
1½ cups chicken stock
½ cup dry white wine
1 bayleaf
2 tablespoons plain flour kneaded with 1 table-
    spoon butter
5 large tomatoes, skinned, seeded and chopped
½ cup plain yoghurt
3 tablespoons chopped parsley

Heat the butter in a heavy-based casserole and brown the lamb for about 5 minutes, then add the onions and cook for a further 5 minutes, stirring occasionally. Draw the pan to one side and add the paprika, garlic, tomato paste and some seasoning. Stir all together and pour in the wine and the stock. Add the bayleaf, stir well, cover and simmer slowly for almost an hour or until the meat is tender. Stir from time to time to prevent the meat sticking to the base. You can now leave it to cool and then keep in the fridge to re-heat later, or you can carry straight on to the end.

Bring the stew to a simmering heat and gradually stir in the flour/butter mixture (*beurre manié*) bit by bit, and keep stirring until the liquid thickens. Continue simmering for a few minutes to get rid of the raw flour taste. Sprinkle over the top the chopped tomatoes, then decoratively spoon over the yoghurt and finally sprinkle with the parsley. Take to table as the effect is very attractive, and ladle on to heated plates.

NOTE   When making something like this, you may think that it has a very lamby smell until the tomatoes, yoghurt and parsley become mixed in with the hot lamb and paprika as you are serving it, when the dish takes on a different smell and, we can guarantee, a most delicious taste as well.

LAMB AND APPLE PIE.
Serves 4–6

Here is a tasty way to use up some left-over cooked lamb, which makes a change from Shepherd's Pie. If you wish, you may use ready-made shortcrust or flaky pastry to top the pie. The apples are best if they are on the tart side. Should you happen to have some lamb stock or left-over thin lamb gravy, use it. Failing that use chicken stock. At a pinch you can use stock powder or cubes mixed with a little water but we are not too keen for this dish; a good tinned consommé is better. And please don't mince the lamb and bacon too fine. Plain boiled potatoes and a green vegetable are best with this pie.

> $1\frac{1}{2}$ *cups cooked minced lamb*
> $\frac{1}{2}$ *cup minced ham or cooked bacon*
> *1 large onion, thinly sliced*
> *2 tart apples, peeled, cored and thinly sliced*

A little salt and freshly ground black pepper
$\frac{1}{4}$ *teaspoon ground dried rosemary*
$\frac{1}{4}$ *teaspoon ground dried sage*
$\frac{3}{4}$ *cup chicken stock or thin gravy*
1 *tablespoon tomato paste*
Enough shortcrust or flaky pastry to cover
Beaten egg to glaze

Arrange the meats, onion and apple in alternate layers into an 8 inch buttered dish, sprinkling each layer with the herbs and seasoning because you want the herbs distributed throughout and not in one lot. Mix the stock or gravy with the tomato paste and pour over. Cover with the rolled out pastry and place in the fridge while you heat the oven to Gas Mark 6 (400°F, 200°C). Make a hole in the middle of the pastry to let the steam escape and brush with the beaten egg. Bake in the centre of the oven for 20–25 minutes until well browned.

LAMB COOKED IN RED WINE
Serves 6–8

Should you be a traditionalist then this may not be to your taste. If, on the other hand, you like robust flavours, then you will enjoy it tremendously. You do really need a casserole with a tight-fitting lid that will just hold the leg of lamb without too much excess space around it. Failing that, use a baking tin and cover the top with a double thickness of foil. As with any dish in which we use wine, the choice should be for a good wine that you would normally drink yourself, not a cheap wine just for cooking purposes. A good claret or burgundy is best here.

> About a 2 kilo (4½lb) leg of lamb
> 3 cloves garlic cut into slivers
> A little melted butter
> Some salt and freshly ground black pepper
> ½ teaspoon ground ginger
> 50 grams (2 oz) butter
> 2 onions, roughly chopped
> 2 carrots, roughly chopped
> 4 sprigs fresh thyme or ½ teaspoon dried
> 1½ cups good claret or burgundy

Make small slits in the lamb and insert the garlic slivers. Brush with a little melted butter and sprinkle all over with the salt, pepper and ground ginger. Melt the 50 grams (2 oz) butter in the chosen casserole or baking dish and gently cook the onions and carrots until the onions are golden. Place the thyme over the vegetables and then put the lamb on top. Roast uncovered at Gas Mark 7 (425°F, 220°C) for 20 minutes. Remove from the oven and reduce the heat to Gas Mark 4 (350°F, 180°C). Pour over the wine and cover the casserole or dish with the lid or foil. Cook for a further 1 hour, basting three or four times. Remove the lamb to a plate and keep warm. Strain the juices into a small pan and boil briskly until reduced by one third. Spoon off excess fat and correct seasoning. Carve the meat and serve the sauce in a heated sauceboat. Serve with plain boiled potatoes and plain steamed carrots.

BRAISED RABBIT IN RED WINE
Serves 4

Every time that we have cooked rabbit on television the audience in the studio have made comments under their breaths. Why people have an aversion to it is beyond us as it is a truly delicious meat, and when cooked ahead of time is a better-behaved meat than chicken, as the latter can become overcooked and stringy at times. We would warn you that when boiling up the wine (and don't forget – the better the wine, the better the result) the aroma doesn't smell as good as one would hope, but don't be put off by this as the taste when cooked is truly magnificent. You may substitute chicken pieces, such as thighs or drumsticks, for the rabbit but cut back the cooking time by about 20 minutes.

1 large rabbit cut into serving pieces
250 grams (9 oz) thick fatty bacon, finely chopped
$\frac{1}{2}$ teaspoon each salt and freshly ground black pepper
2 tablespoons plain flour
1 medium onion, finely chopped
2 cloves garlic, finely chopped
1 cup good dry red wine
1 cup good chicken stock
2 tablespoons cognac or brandy
1 heaped tablespoon redcurrant jelly
1 large bayleaf
$\frac{1}{2}$ teaspoon dried crushed rosemary
$\frac{1}{2}$ teaspoon dried thyme
Juice of half a lemon

Cook the bacon over fairly high heat in a heavy-based casserole until crisp. Remove with a slotted spoon and keep to one side. Rinse the rabbit portions under cold water and pat dry. Sprinkle with the salt and pepper and then dust with the flour. Sauté in the bacon fat that remains in the casserole until lightly browned over a moderate heat. Do this a few pieces at a time so as to give yourself room to move them around. Remove the pieces as they are browned to a plate. Now cook the onion and garlic in the casserole over gentle heat. As there is very little fat left in the casserole it is best to cook the onions with the lid on. Stir them from time to time until they are soft but not browned. Now add the wine and the chicken stock and bring to the boil, while stirring up any residue of flour that may be stuck to the bottom of the casserole. This is when the smell might be a bit off-putting. Stir in the cognac, jelly, bayleaf, rosemary and thyme, and return the rabbit pieces, together with any juices that may have exuded from them, to the casserole. Add the crisp bacon, cover with the lid and simmer very gently for $1\frac{1}{2}$ hours or until tender, stirring once or twice during that time. When cooked, remove the bayleaf, and take out the rabbit pieces and keep them warm. Boil down the juices in the casserole to make a sauce, add the lemon juice and then check the seasoning – it should err on the peppery side. Serve with plain steamed potatoes with the sauce poured over the rabbit, and a green vegetable on a separate side plate.

NOTE You may prefer to prepare up to the 1½-hour cooking stage on top of your stove, cover and then finish off in the oven. In which case cook at Gas Mark 3 (325°F, 170°C) in the lower centre of the oven for about the same time as on top of the stove. You will still have to finish boiling down the juices to make the sauce on top, however.

PORK STROGANOFF
Serves 4

We find this a very 'comforting' dish. It is usual to use fillet of beef but we often use pork fillets for a change. It can be served with noodles, steamed or mashed potatoes, or rice. We also like a vegetable such as broccoli or green beans served on a separate plate so that the sauce doesn't run into them. We find it best to cook the sauce part and the meat individually and then combine both just prior to serving. We have suggested 500 grams (18 oz) of pork fillet but if you wish you can add extra, up to, but not exceeding 750 grams (1½ lb). You can cut the pork fillet into slices or strips, but which ever you prefer they must be thin so that they cook quickly.

> *500 grams (18 oz) trimmed pork fillet*
> *50 grams (2 oz) unsalted butter*
> *2 medium onions, finely chopped*
> *1 tablespoon tomato purée or paste*
> *1 large clove garlic, crushed*

1 tablespoon arrowroot
1½ cups good beef stock (see note at end)
2 teaspoons Worcestershire sauce
200 grams (7 oz) small mushrooms, thinly sliced
A little salt and freshly ground pepper
1 cup sour cream

Trim any fat and sinew from the fillet and cut into thin strips or slices. Season with a little salt and pepper and keep covered while you make the sauce. Preferably in a non-stick frying-pan, melt most of the butter and cook the onions until they are soft and golden. Add the tomato purée or paste, garlic and arrowroot and cook, stirring for a couple of minutes. Add the stock, bring to the boil and stir until thickened. Add the Worcestershire sauce and the mushrooms and continue to cook over gentle heat for about 5 minutes. While this is gently simmering, cook the prepared fillet in just a hint of butter until the pieces change colour, about 5 minutes also. Pour the sour cream into the sauce, stir until heated through and add the pork, continue to heat until just below boiling point, and serve immediately.

NOTE We suggest a good, well-flavoured beef stock rather than some chicken stock. You can certainly use the latter if you wish, but we prefer beef because it gives a better colour to the end result and in our opinion it improves the flavour. The tomato paste gives the finished dish a slightly sharp taste, which again we also like, so much so that just prior to serving we also add a good squeeze of lemon juice to

sharpen it even further. You should not have any
trouble even if the sauce does boil slightly after you
have added the sour cream because the arrowroot
will help to stabilize it.

PORK CHOPS WITH APRICOTS
Serves 4

This is terribly easy and can be extended by mul-
tiplying the ingredients to suit the number of people
to be served. However the chops need to be quite
thick; thin ones will not do. You can ring the
changes on taste by using cooked apple slices or
soaked and stoned prunes. The important thing,
which will save you a hassle later, is to line your
baking dish with a double thickness of heavy-duty
foil as the ginger ale, because of its sugar content,
makes quite a mess on the base of an ordinary
baking dish. This dish can be considered a 'mini'
roast.

> 4 thick pork chops
> 12 large dried apricots, soaked for several hours
>   and drained
> 9 sprigs fresh thyme or 1 teaspoon dried
> A little salt and freshly ground black pepper
> 1 small bottle of ginger ale

You may want to trim some of the fat from the
chops, in which case you will have to remove the
rind. Place a chop down flat and place four of the

apricots along its length. Place three sprigs of thyme or a third of the dried thyme on top of the apricots, and finally sprinkle with a little salt and pepper. Place another chop on top, lying the same way as the one underneath, and again the apricots, thyme, salt and pepper. Do this until you have a four-decker pork 'sandwich'. Pin together to secure with long skewers or, better still, tie it with fine string into a 'parcel'. Place in your foil-lined baking dish and pour over the ginger ale. Bake at Gas Mark 5 (375°F, 190°C) in the middle of the oven for about 1 hour, basting frequently. Should the top start to over colour, lay another sheet of foil over the chops to protect them. Serve with very plain vegetables as they are rather rich.

NOTE   If you have not removed the rind, sometimes you get a very nice crackling automatically, or you can pop the chops under a grill to make the skin crackle. This doesn't always work with every chop we have used in the past, so don't worry if it doesn't with yours.

CASSEROLE OF DUCK WITH PAPRIKA
Serves 6–8

First you need a heavy casserole that can be used on top of the stove and then in the oven. The better the wine in this dish the better the end result. As we have always said in the past, use the same wine to cook this dish as you will drink with it when served.

Another important point is to make sure that the paprika is fresh and not some old stock that you have had lying around in the back of your store cupboard. It is worth buying fresh paprika to get the best taste from this meal. Served with some savoury flavoured rice, with a green salad to follow, you will find this a superb way of cooking duck.

> 45 grams (1½ oz) butter
> 2 onions, finely chopped
> 3 large cloves garlic, finely chopped
> 1 large plump duck
> 2 tablespoons plain flour
> 1 tablespoon fresh paprika
> 1 cup good red wine, either burgundy or claret
> A little salt and freshly ground black pepper
> 5 large tomatoes, skinned and roughly chopped.

Melt the butter in a large casserole and fry the onions and the garlic for a few minutes. Add the duck and brown as much as you can on all sides, then remove the duck from the casserole. Sprinkle the flour and the paprika over the onions, stir together then add the wine to make a thickish sauce. Season with a little salt and pepper then return the duck to the casserole, cover with the tomatoes, then put on the lid. Place in the middle of the oven preset to Gas Mark 3 (325°F, 170°C) and cook until tender, approx. 1½–2 hours depending on the quality and age of the duck. Remove the duck and carve into 6–8 portions, depending on the size, and keep hot. Remove excess fat from the sauce, and if needed reduce over fairly high heat, stirring all the time, until it thickens. Spoon over the duck and serve straight away.

NOTE Because carving can take a while and it is not that easy, we nearly always joint the duck before we cook it, which makes it easier to brown and serve. Reduce the cooking times by about ½ hour if you decide to joint it first.

LEMON CASSEROLED CHICKENS
Serves 4

Simple recipes usually taste really good, but they rely very much on the quality of the produce you use. This recipe is a case in point. You need two very good small birds that are just large enough so that when cut in half, each half will be adequate for one person. You will also need a casserole that will accommodate the birds without too much extra space and which has a tight-fitting lid as, cooked on a fairly low heat, they are really being steamed rather than roasted. If you think your lid is not tight enough to retain the moisture, then place a double thickness of foil on top, press it well around the sides of the casserole before placing on the lid.

2 small fresh chickens
A little salt and freshly ground black pepper
50 grams (2 oz) clarified butter or 2 tablespoons
    virgin olive oil
1 large lemon, cut in half

4 more tablespoons virgin olive oil
½ cup good chicken stock
Juice of 1 large lemon
1 tablespoon finely chopped parsley

Rinse both birds and pat dry inside and out with kitchen paper. Sprinkle the cavities with a little salt and pepper and place into each bird half the butter, or 1 tablespoon of oil, and half a lemon. Truss with some string to keep them compact while cooking. In a heavy-based casserole that has a tight-fitting lid brown the birds, one at a time, over moderate heat in the 4 tablespoons of oil. When both are browned, place them side by side in the casserole, breast side up. Add the chicken stock, lemon juice and parsley. Spoon a little of this over each bird and sprinkle with a little freshly ground black pepper. Cover with the lid (or foil and lid), and cook in the lower portion of the oven set at Gas Mark 2 (300°F, 160°C) for between 1¼ and 1¾ hours. Check to see if they are done after the first time given, by pricking the thigh to see if the juices run clear. If they are not cooked, baste and cover and cook for a while longer until ready. The time really depends on the quality of the birds. Remove from the casserole, and leave in a warm place for 10 minutes. Cut off the string, and cut the birds in half lengthwise through the breast and back. As the sauce remaining in the casserole will be fatty, do not use. Just serve them plain with buttered, parsleyed, steamed small potatoes and a green vegetable such as beans or broccoli, steamed and tossed in a little butter.

CHICKEN LIVERS AND WHITE GRAPES
Serves 6

This is a dish that we don't have that often, not because of the shortage of chicken livers but the fact that we only make it when seedless green grapes are on the market. As it is relatively rich we suggest that you serve it with a green salad with a lemony dressing or a green vegetable such as broccoli or asparagus. Use a baguette cut into long diagonal slices for the bread and choose one that has some whole grains rather than just plain white.

> *750 grams (1¾ lb) chicken livers*
> *A little salt and freshly ground black pepper*
> *3 tablespoons butter*
> *6 long thickish slices bread*
> *Some melted clarified butter*
> *½ cup madeira or port*
> *450 grams (1 lb) white seedless grapes*

Rinse and trim the livers, then cut into pieces. Season with a little salt and pepper and leave to one side. Brush both sides of the bread with some melted clarified butter and place on a metal oven tray. Bake until golden brown at Gas Mark 6 (400°F, 200°C) for about 8 minutes, turning the slices over once in that time. Place on crumpled kitchen paper and keep warm. Melt the butter in a heavy-based pan and add the livers. Do this on a fairly high heat and stir the livers around with a wooden spoon to cook all sides of them. Don't, however, overcook; you still want them pink on the inside. This will only take

about 5 minutes maximum. With a slotted spoon
remove the livers to a plate or bowl and keep warm
also. Pour the madeira or port into the pan and boil
until reduced to a light syrup consistency. Add the
grapes and swirl around to heat them through.
Place one slice of the bread on each individual
serving plate, divide the livers equally on the bread
slices; likewise with the grapes and sauce.

NOTE When we originally used this recipe, we
used to add several tablespoons of cold butter to the
sauce and swirl it around to make it more unctuous,
but we have stopped doing that now.

LIVER WITH ORANGE SAUCE
Serves 4–6

Use either lamb or calves liver for this but certainly
not ox. Making use of flavour apéritifs such as
sherry, vermouth or dubonnet can alter the taste of
the finished dish quite considerably, as can madeira,
sweet or dry. Served with an in-season green vegetable and gorgeous creamy mashed potatoes, this is
very good for the chillier days of the year. As the
liver has to be cut into thin slices you might like to
try placing it in the freezer until it is partially frozen,
as we do. This makes the job of slicing so much
easier. Never overcook.

> 500 grams (18 oz) liver
> Seasoned flour

2 onions, finely chopped
2 cloves garlic, finely chopped
3 tablespoons butter
1 tablespoon plain oil
½ cup dubonnet, vermouth etc.
Juice of half an orange (the whole if not too juicy)
3 tablespoons finely chopped parsley
Grated rind of a lemon and an orange
Salt and finely ground black pepper to taste

Wash and trim the liver and cut into very thin slices, then dust with the seasoned flour. Shake off the excess and place the liver to one side. Fry the onion and the garlic in the butter and oil in a heavy-based frying-pan until soft and lightly coloured. Add the sliced liver and, stirring all the time, cook for about 3–4 minutes until coloured. With a slotted spoon place the liver and onions on a serving dish and keep hot. This is why you cook the liver so little as it will continue to cook slightly while you make the sauce. Pour into the pan the vermouth or dubonnet etc., and boil rapidly to reduce by half. Mix in most of the parsley, lemon and orange rind, keeping a little back for decoration. Heat through and pour over the liver and onions. Sprinkle with the reserved parsley and rinds and serve immediately.

HONEY-COATED CHICKEN WITH
THYME AND MINT CREAM SAUCE
Serves 4

When a friend of ours came to visit from New York she brought this recipe with her as she thought we might be interested. One wet day we got into the kitchen and this was the end result. We must explain that there is one messy bit, when you drain the chicken after it has been in the marinade and then coat it with seasoned flour, so have plenty of paper towels available for draining and then dusting. She recommended that we fry the chicken in a mixture of lard and oil, but we prefer oil, so choose a bland-flavoured oil such as safflower. We also use a non-stick frying-pan to fry the chicken and also to make the sauce in later.

> 1 large chicken cut into serving pieces enough for 4
> $\frac{1}{2}$ cup liquid honey
> 3 tablespoons fruit-flavoured vinegar (raspberry) or cider
> $\frac{1}{2}$ cup plain flour
> 1 teaspoon salt
> 8 grindings black pepper
> $\frac{1}{2}$ to $\frac{3}{4}$ cup safflower (or similar) oil
> $\frac{1}{2}$ cup dry white wine
> $\frac{1}{2}$ cup good chicken stock
> 1 cup cream
> $1\frac{1}{2}$ tablespoons finely chopped mint
> 1 teaspoon dried thyme or 1 tablespoon freshly chopped

1 teaspoon finely grated lemon rind
2 tablespoons reserved marinade
Salt and pepper to taste

Place the chicken pieces in a large glass or ceramic bowl. Warm the honey and vinegar together and pour over the chicken. We generally do this in a small glass bowl in the microwave. Leave the chicken in the marinade for at least 3 hours, turning it occasionally to coat the pieces. Take the chicken out of the marinade, letting the liquid drip off, then place on paper towels to drain. Mix the flour and salt and pepper together and coat the chicken pieces lightly. Heat the oil in a large non-stick frying-pan and fry the coated chicken pieces over a moderate heat until well browned, turning them frequently. This will take about 20 minutes. While they are cooking, strain the marinade through a sieve and reserve 2 tablespoons. When all the chicken pieces are cooked, keep warm in the oven. Drain the oil and fat from the pan leaving only the little brown bits that may have stuck to the base (with a non-stick this is unlikely), and pour in the wine and the chicken stock. Boil until reduced by half. Add the cream, mint, thyme, lemon rind and marinade (2 tablespoons) and keep boiling until the sauce will coat the back of a spoon. Check for seasoning and pour into a heated sauceboat to serve with the chicken. You can pass the sauce through a sieve if you wish to hold back the bits, but we generally don't as it has a lovely speckled appearance. Served with a side plate of freshly cooked asparagus with a dab of butter and

a little squeeze of lemon juice it is a really gorgeous
dish.

SESAME-FLAVOURED CHICKEN BREASTS
Serves 4

This can be served cold without the sauce as part of
a salad, or served on some rice with the sauce as
part of a Chinese meal or on its own for a light
middle course.

> 2 whole chicken breasts
> 1 teaspoon cornflour
> 1 egg white
> 2 tablespoons sesame seeds, crushed
> 2 tablespoons peanut oil
> Several drops sesame seed oil
> 1 cup chicken stock
> 1 teaspoon arrowroot
> A little salt and pepper to taste or soy sauce (see
> note below)

Skin the chicken breasts and remove any bone if
not already done. Cut each one in half lengthwise to
make four portions. Beat the egg white and cornflour together and coat the breasts in it. Put the
crushed sesame seeds (do this in a pestle and mortar)
on a shallow plate and lightly coat both sides of the
drained chicken breasts with them. Use more
crushed sesame seeds if you want a thicker coating.
Heat the peanut oil and sesame oil together in a

heavy-based frying-pan and cook the breasts over a moderate heat for about 3 minutes on either side. If you want to stop here and serve them cold, cook for 5 minutes on either side and remove. If you are continuing to the end of the recipe, mix the chicken stock and arrowroot together and add to the pan, stir around and poach the chicken breasts in this sauce for about another 3 minutes, turning them once during that time. Place each on to a plate with some cooked rice and spoon the sauce over them.

NOTE   We mentioned a little salt and pepper. You can add this to the sauce, but we prefer to add at table or alternatively if it is to be served as part of a Chinese meal then we cut the chicken into pieces and just before serving splash over some light soy sauce instead of using salt.

CHINESE CRISP-SKINNED CHICKEN
Serves 2

This is very easy to do, but you must have an oven that is well vented as there is often quite a bit of smoking near the end of the cooking time; don't let this put you off. The chicken is cooked on the wire rack in the oven, with a tray set on the lower rack underneath to catch any drips. Use a chicken that is fairly small, but one that will serve two people when split in half lengthwise. The quantities for the mixture that goes inside the bird is enough for one chicken only but if you want to make this recipe for more than two people, multiply the quantities accordingly. It is best eaten with a knife and your fingers, with a fingerbowl by the side. If you love crispy skin you will adore this. A simple green salad and a simple dessert would complete the meal.

> 3 whole spring onions, chopped
> 2 stalks celery, chopped
> 1 bayleaf, crumbled
> 2 cloves garlic, chopped
> A good pinch Chinese 5 spices or allspice
> 1 tablespoon chopped green ginger
> 1 small chicken
> A little peanut oil
> A heaped teaspoon of salt

Place all the ingredients except the chicken, oil and salt into a saucepan with 3 cups of water. Boil for 5 minutes. Place the chicken in a large bowl in a sink, and using a sieve, pour the boiling water all over the chicken, making sure that the water has come in contact with all the skin. Drain the chicken and place all the vegetables that were trapped in the sieve inside the bird's cavity. These act as a flavouring and also keep the bird moist. Heat the oven to Gas Mark 4 (350°F, 180°C), and place the baking tin on the lower rungs as described. Put a good teaspoon of salt into the palm of one hand and add about 2 tablespoons oil, rub together in both hands and then rub over the skin of the chicken, coating the whole surface. Place on the rungs above the tin, breast side up and bake for about 1 hour or until the chicken is golden brown and crisp. Cut in half and discard the vegetables.

CHINESE-STYLE CHICKEN AND PINEAPPLE WITH HONEY
Serves 4 or more

This is another of our favourite tasty simple Chinese-style dishes which again can be cooked in a large shallow pan but is best cooked in a wok. You can use a whole chicken or chicken pieces cut up into smallish chunky pieces with a cleaver. We have cooked it using cut-up chicken breasts, but the addition of the bone being left in the chicken pieces gives a much better taste. Use peanut oil for deep frying and then strain through a very fine sieve and keep for another time. However, you need a fair amount of oil, and this is where the wok comes into its own because for this you only need about $1\frac{1}{2}$ cups to deep fry the chicken. We make no apologies for using tinned pineapple pieces either. As with most Chinese dishes, have everything cut up and prepared before starting to cook. Serve this over plain boiled rice.

*1 chicken, or chicken pieces, weighing 1.5 kilos
    (approx. $3\frac{1}{2}$ lb)*
Cornflour for dusting
1 to $1\frac{1}{2}$ cups peanut oil for deep frying
2 cloves garlic, crushed
1inch piece of fresh ginger, grated
425 grams (17 oz) tin pineapple pieces, drained
1 red pepper, seeded and cubed
$1\frac{1}{2}$ cups chicken stock
2 teaspoons arrowroot
1 tablespoon runny honey

A little salt
2 teaspoons sesame oil
6 spring onions, sliced diagonally

If using a whole chicken cut up into pieces and dust the pieces lightly with cornflour. Fry in batches in the hot peanut oil in a wok until golden brown, about 5 minutes per batch. Remove with a slotted spoon as they are cooked and drain on crumpled kitchen paper. Drain off the oil through a sieve into a heatproof container, leaving about 2 tablespoons oil in the wok. Add the garlic and ginger and cook for 1 minute then add the pineapple pieces and red pepper and toss quickly over high heat for 2 minutes. Remove from wok. Mix the arrowroot with the stock and put with the honey, salt and sesame oil in the wok, stirring until the sauce boils and thickens. Return the chicken, pineapple and red pepper to the wok and toss the mixture over high heat until the chicken heats through, about 3 minutes. Toss in the spring onions, stir together and serve. It will serve more than four people if the dish becomes part of a Chinese meal.

NOTE   If you haven't a red pepper available use a green one but blanch it briefly, after you have seeded it and cut into cubes, in boiling water for a minute before using. We often use a red and a green pepper and sometimes add a yellow one too, as we like the extra peppers in this dish.

SICHUAN BEEF AND BEANCURD
Serves 4 or more

Most dishes that come from the Sichuan area are
hot and spicy; this is no exception. Although this
can be cooked in a deep, heavy-based pan it is better
done in a wok. If you have no salted black beans,
then you can use a tablespoon of black-bean sauce.
The chilli paste or purée must be hot, but again you
can lessen the strength by using a milder flavoured
tomato-based chilli sauce, we personally don't as
we like it very fiery. Also, Sichuan pepper can be
readily purchased from most stores that stock a good
range of Oriental supplies and it is quite different
from other peppers. As with all Chinese dishes, have
everything prepared before you commence cooking.
Serve over a fragrant plain boiled rice such as
Jasmine.

3 blocks of beancurd, about 750 grams (1¾ lb) total
1 teaspoon peanut oil
200 grams (7 oz) lean minced beef
¼ teaspoon salt
*1 teaspoon salted black beans, or 1 tablespoon
   black bean sauce*
1 tablespoon chilli paste
½ cup beef stock
3 spring onions, sliced
1 tablespoon dark soy sauce
1 tablespoon arrowroot mixed with ¼ cup water
Freshly ground Sichuan pepper

Cut the bean curd into half-inch cubes, blanch in

boiling water for 2 minutes and drain. Heat peanut
oil in a wok and stir fry the beef over high heat until
well browned. This takes a fair while because it
turns opaque, emits juices then starts to become
drier and eventually goes a deep brown. Add salt,
then crushed beans or bean sauce, mix well and
add chilli, stirring all the time until you start to
'smell' the chilli – it gets up your nostrils. Now add
stock and bean curd and spring onions, lower heat
and cook for 3 minutes. Add soy and the arrowroot
mixture, stir gently together for 1 minute more and
serve over rice. If it is part of a full Chinese meal it
will serve more than four people.

BREASTS OF CHICKEN WITH CHILLI AND HONEY SAUCE
Serves 6–8

We both seem to have a liking for choosing things
that are either easy or done ahead of time. This dish
falls into the latter and can be made a day in advance. As with most recipes of an Oriental persuasion
there is a lot of preparatory work but once that is
over the cooking is easy and the taste scrumptious.
The amount of chilli given may seem very bland to
some people's taste, but you can add extra before
you finally serve it if you are adding a hot chilli
sauce to the mixture. If you use chilli powder you
will have to mix it in with a little water and simmer
the sauce for an extra 2–3 minutes to get rid of that
powdery taste.

4 chicken breasts, skinned and boned and divided
   in half
250 grams (9 oz) minced pork
250 grams (9 oz) prawns or shrimps (tinned can
   be used)
6 spring onions
1 inch piece of green ginger, peeled
250 gram (9 oz) water chestnuts (tinned)
2 sticks celery
1 tablespoon gin
1 egg yolk
2 teaspoons light soy sauce
A little salt and pepper
Some plain flour
2 eggs
$\frac{1}{4}$ cup milk
3 cups fresh breadcrumbs
Peanut oil for frying
4 more spring onions, sliced diagonally

Chilli and Honey Sauce

$\frac{1}{2}$ cup tomato sauce
2 tablespoons white vinegar
$\frac{1}{3}$ cup honey
1 tablespoon dark soy sauce
1 tablespoon chilli sauce or $\frac{1}{2}$ teaspoon chilli powder
2 tablespoons dry sherry
1 cup chicken stock (or 1 cup water and 1 teaspoon
   stock powder)
1 tablespoon arrowroot

Pound the 8 pieces of chicken breasts between two pieces of heavy waxed paper until fairly thin. Put the pork mince in a large glass or china bowl, add the prawns, spring onions, ginger, drained water chestnuts and celery, which you have chopped very finely by hand or in a food processor. Mix together well, then add the gin, egg yolk, soy sauce and seasoning, and mix with either a wooden spoon or your hands, a bit messy but all the ingredients must be well mixed. To mix really well, take out the mixture with your hands and throw it back into the bowl, do this several times until the whole thing becomes a glutinous mass. Lay the chicken breasts out and divide the pork mixture evenly between them, spreading it to the edges of the chicken. Dust each portion lightly with flour on both sides. Beat eggs and milk well in a shallow dish, and dip each chicken piece into the egg and milk mixture, to coat both sides and then shake off the excess gently. Now dip them into the breadcrumbs, coating both sides lightly. Lay on a flat dish or plate, cover, and pop in the fridge for at least 1 hour or overnight. Heat some peanut oil in a shallow pan or preferably a wok and fry each chicken piece on both sides until light golden brown. Do not have the oil too hot or they will brown before the chicken is cooked. Each piece, and you can do several at a time, will take about 4–5 minutes. Drain the chicken on crumpled paper and keep warm while you cook the next batch. When all of it is cooked, cut the chicken pieces into slices cross-wise about 2 inches wide, and mound up on a heated serving dish. Pour the

chilli sauce over and sprinkle with the four sliced
spring onions.

The chilli sauce is very simple to make. Just whisk
all the ingredients together in a medium-sized
saucepan over moderate heat and simmer until it
reaches boiling point. Lower the heat and simmer
gently still whisking occasionally for about 4
minutes.

NOTE   When we are frying the chicken, we often
add several shakes of sesame oil to the peanut oil; it
gives it a lovely indefinable flavour. If you are a
freak for sesame oil, as we are, you can also add a
little to your sauce; but don't overdo it in either
instance as sesame is quite strong in flavour and
can take over. All you need serve with this dish is a
bowl of plain rice per person and, if you feel inclined,
afterwards a simple salad.

QUICK CURRIED CHICKEN BREASTS
WITH MANGO SAUCE
Serves 4

This was devised at the last moment to fill a gap
when we were doing our first BBC show. It really
wasn't a recipe because it was so simple; however
hundreds of our viewers requested it. We use
Basmati rice which comes from India and has a
wonderful flavour but you could use a long grain or
brown rice if you wish. The curry paste can be any
of the reputable proprietary brands. You may choose

a mild, medium or hot paste, according to your own palate.

> 2 whole chicken breasts, skinned and boned
> 4–8 teaspoons curry paste
> 3 tablespoons clarified butter
> 1 medium tin of mango slices
> ½–1 teaspoon Garam Masala
> 3 cups of cooked rice

Cut the two chicken breasts down the centre to give four pieces. Spread one side only with the chosen curry paste. Melt the butter in a heavy-based pan, preferably large enough to hold the four chicken breasts. Place the chicken non-curry side down and gently cook over a moderate heat for about 3 minutes, turn and cook 2 minutes on the curry paste side and then turn again for a further minute. While these are cooking, tip the tin of mangoes and the juice into a medium-sized saucepan and add the Garam Masala according to your own taste. Stir and heat through. Divide the cooked rice on to four heated serving plates, place a cooked chicken breast on top and spoon over the mango slices with just a little of the juice. Serve accompanied with pop-padoms and other relishes, tomatoes, peanuts, chutneys, cucumber in yoghurt and mint etc.

SPICY PARMESAN DRUMSTICKS
Serves 4

As chicken portions can be purchased practically anywhere, these make a very tasty middle course, or they can be used for a buffet party. We always buy our Parmesan cheese in a block and then grate it, as required, by dropping thin slices down the feed tube of a food processor while the motor and steel blade are turning. This gives a 'granular' texture which is better than ordinary grated, and the flavour is more pronounced than using ready-grated Parmesan from a packet; it's cheaper too. This recipe can be prepared up to a day in advance of cooking, which is a great time-saver when you are giving a dinner or lunch party.

> 12 chicken drumsticks
> 2 thick slices bread, crusts removed, turned into
>   crumbs
> 2 cloves garlic, crushed
> Grated rind of a lemon
> 1 teaspoon salt
> $\frac{1}{2}$ teaspoon freshly ground black pepper
> 1 teaspoon dried rosemary, pounded or already
>   powdered
> $\frac{1}{4}$ teaspoon of cayenne or chilli powder
> About 100 grams (4 oz) melted butter
> 4 rounded tablespoonfuls parmesan cheese

Rinse and pat dry the drumsticks. Mix all the other ingredients, with the exception of the butter, in a large shallow bowl. Brush each chicken piece with melted butter and coat with the crumb mixture in the bowl, making sure you have them well coated. Place on a plate, cover and chill for at least an hour. Lightly butter an ovenproof dish large enough to hold the drumsticks in a single layer. Place the drumsticks in the dish and drizzle with any remaining butter. Bake Gas Mark 7 (425°F, 200–210°C) for about 35–40 minutes or until well browned. Serve with a green vegetable.

DUCK BREASTS IN PASTRY
Serves 8

As duck has such a lovely taste it is good to have recipes that include it which are not only flavoursome but also economical. This is one such recipe, and into the bargain it can be prepared a day ahead. As we only use the duck breasts for this recipe we include the duck pâté that is made from the rest of the birds on page 12 in the 'Beginnings' section of the book. However, because we have suggested a very good orange-flavoured sauce to go with the duck breast in pastry, which has the basis of a simple Espagnole sauce, we will begin with both sauces before we get down to the duck.

Simple Espagnole Sauce

This is certainly best made with your own beef stock, but we have used tins of beef consommé on odd occasions. One thing that does *not* work, however, is commercial beef-stock powder or cubes which

have a high salt content and, because this sauce is
reduced, would make the end result far too salty.

NOTE   Once you have made the sauce and strained
it, you may keep it in the fridge for up to 3 days or
freeze for later use.

> *2 tablespoons butter or beef dripping*
> *1 large carrot, finely chopped*
> *1 large onion, finely chopped*
> *1 large rasher of bacon, finely diced*
> *2 tablespoons plain flour*
> *2 cups beef stock (explained above)*
> *Bouquet garni*
> *2 tablespoons tomato paste*
> *Freshly ground black pepper*

In a heavy-based saucepan with a good-fitting lid,
melt the butter or beef dripping and add the carrot,
onion and bacon. Cook these over a medium heat
for about 10 minutes or until lightly browned,
stirring occasionally. Blend in the flour and stir until
it colours, but don't let it burn. Add 1½ cups of the
stock and cook for 3 minutes, stirring all the time
until it has thickened. Add the bouquet garni, cover
with the lid and simmer on the lowest heat for 30
minutes, stirring several times to make sure that it
doesn't catch. Add the remaining half cup of stock
and the tomato paste, cover and simmer again
for another 30 minutes on the lowest heat, this
time stirring more frequently. Strain through a
very fine sieve, pressing the vegetables with the
back of a wooden spoon to extract their juices.

Adjust seasoning. This makes about 1½ cups.

The Orange Flavoured Sauce

> 1 to 1½ cups Espagnole sauce (see above)
> Finely grated rind and juice of 1 orange
> Juice of ½ lemon
> ¼ cup good red wine or port
> 2 tablespoons redcurrant jelly

Place all the ingredients together in a saucepan and heat through, stirring all the time. Serve in a heated sauceboat. Enough for 8 servings.

Now we go back to the duck breasts themselves.

> 2 plump ducks
> 2 duck or chicken livers
> 3 rashers of lean bacon, chopped
> 1 medium onion, finely chopped
> Finely grated rind of 1 orange
> 2 tablespoons of butter
> 2 tablespoons finely chopped green olives (about 6)
> 1 tablespoon brandy
> About 500 grams (18 oz) of prepared pastry (puff,
>   flaky or filo)
> 1 egg beaten with 1 tablespoon water

Pre-heat the oven to Gas Mark 6 (400°F, 200°C) and roast the ducks in a baking tin on a rack for 50 to 60 minutes. Remove from the oven and leave to cool. Sauté the chopped duck or chicken livers, bacon, onion and orange rind in the butter for 5 minutes. Add the chopped olives and the brandy and cook for another minute. Leave to cool. Skin the ducks and carve the breasts off in two whole pieces. Cut each piece in half along its length, giving you eight pieces. Roll out the puff or flaky pastry fairly thinly and cut into eight pieces large enough to surround the duck pieces and some filling. If using the filo, you will need eight large sheets. Brush some melted butter on four of them and place the other four on top, giving you four sets of two thicknesses. Cut each of the double layers in half crosswise to give you eight pieces. Place one piece of duck on to each piece of pastry and divide the filling on top of each duck piece equally. Moisten the edges with some water and wrap each piece up envelope style, making sure the edges are sealed. Place the packages seam side down on a lightly buttered baking tray and brush with the beaten egg to glaze. Bake in a pre-heated oven at Gas Mark 6 (400°F, 200°C) for about 20 minutes until golden brown, slightly less if using the filo. Serve with the Orange-flavoured Sauce and a green vegetable.

NOTE The duck can be prepared up to wrapping and sealing in the pastry, and kept in the fridge for a maximum of one day. Cook straight from the fridge. Also we have found that if you sprinkle a little cold water over the top of the filo pastry packages just before popping them in the oven it lets the pastry cook through before becoming too brown.

CHICKEN PARCELS WITH CHAMPAGNE AND PUMPKIN SAUCE
Serves 4

This is a very interesting and simple meal for guests. Both the chicken breast parcels and the sauce can be made earlier in the day; the parcels can then be cooked and the sauce re-heated. We usually serve a mixed green salad with a lemony dressing and croutes spread with a very good paté as a beginning with this meal. With this middle course we serve baked spring onions, then we use up the remainder of the champagne to make a Champagne and Orange Sorbet (see page 158), and finally a firm cheese served in slices sprinkled with virgin olive oil and cracked black pepper. You will need to poach the chicken breasts in advance in good chicken stock and leave them to go cold before proceeding with the filo-wrapped parcels.

> 6 dried apricots, soaked until soft
> 1 tablespoon finely chopped parsley
> $\frac{1}{2}$ teaspoon either dried tarragon or thyme
> 1 teaspoon Dijon mustard
> 2 spring onions, finely chopped
> A little salt and freshly ground black pepper
> 2 whole chicken breasts, skinned and boned
> 2 cups good well-flavoured chicken stock
> Maximum of 12 filo pastry sheets (depending on size)
> Melted clarified butter
> 24 spring onions for making ties and for baking (see page 122)

For the Sauce

$\frac{3}{4}$ cup reserved chicken stock, after poaching the
chicken
$\frac{1}{2}$ cup dry champagne
$\frac{1}{2}$ cup puréed pumpkin
$\frac{1}{4}$ cup cream
Seasoning to taste

Drain the soaked apricots and chop fairly fine. Put
into a bowl together with the parsley, dried herb,
mustard, spring onions and a little seasoning. Mix
well, cover and chill. Having removed any skin and
bone from the chicken breasts, also remove the fillets
and keep for another use. Place each whole chicken
breast between two large pieces of clingwrap and
beat with a rolling pin or similar object to flatten
them slightly. Take off the clingwrap and divide the
apricot filling equally between the two whole
breasts, spreading it down the centre. Roll each
breast up and tie fairly tightly in several places to
keep them in shape. Poach in the chicken stock in a
covered casserole for about 20 minutes over a low
heat at a gentle simmer with the lid on the casserole.
Turn them once halfway through the cooking time.
Remove from the heat and leave to go cold in their
stock. Remove from the stock when cold and pass
the stock through a sieve to strain out any solids,
reserve that stock to make the sauce. Remove string
and cut each poached chicken breast in half across
to give four portions. Depending on the size of the
filo pastry sheets you will need three thicknesses per
portion and they should be large enough to encase

each portion, covering them well. Your sheets may be large enough to use cut in half. Butter a sheet of filo with some of the melted clarified butter, lay another sheet on that and brush with butter again and then lay on a third sheet. Place a portion of the chicken, cut side down, in the centre of the buttered sheets and pull up all around to make a casing, similar to wrapping a pudding in cloth. Twist the top around slightly and tie with a piece of string. When you have done the four portions, put in the fridge to chill prior to baking.

To make the sauce, simply put the ¾ cup strained reserved stock into a medium-sized pan together with the champagne and bring to the boil. Stir in the pumpkin purée and simmer until reduced by about a third, then add the cream and simmer for about a minute. Add a little seasoning if necessary. Serve with the cooked chicken parcels.

To cook the parcels. Pre-heat the oven to Gas Mark 6 (400°F, 200°C) and bake for about 20 minutes or until deep golden brown. Remove from the oven, carefully remove string and replace with a green spring onion tie.

To make the ties, and also to bake the spring onions, proceed as follows. Allow six good-sized spring onions per person. Wash and trim the bases leaving the long green ends intact. Take two of the long green ends and split each in half lengthways to give you four long 'ties'. Blanch quickly in boiling water then refresh in cold and lay out on a sheet of paper towel until needed. After removing the string from around the top of the cooked parcels, re-tie with one of these spring onion ties. If long enough, tie in a bow, if not just tie once. Dry the spring onions and lay, preferably in a single layer all in the same direction, in a large flat baking dish. Brush over a little melted clarified butter and sprinkle with some freshly ground black pepper and a little salt. Bake at Gas Mark 6 (400°F, 200°C) for about 8–10 minutes until very hot. Serve with the chicken parcels and the sauce.

CHICKEN SALAD IN A PASTRY CASE
Serves 4–6

This is a very attractive salad dish that is ideal for a light but substantial middle course. You can make the choux pastry case in advance, but we prefer to make it earlier in the day on which the dish is to be served, because, as the case has to be crisp and cool, it is best made not too far in advance. However, having said that, it can be re-crisped in the oven about an hour before it is required to be filled. The salad filling should be made and chilled for at least a couple of hours before it is placed into the choux case; if you put it all in the case and chill the whole thing the case will become soggy.

The Pastry Shell

30 grams (1 oz) butter
$\frac{1}{2}$ teaspoon salt
$\frac{3}{4}$ cup water

$1\frac{1}{4}$ *cups plain flour*
3 large eggs

Place the butter, salt and water into a medium-sized saucepan and bring to the boil. While this is coming to the boil, sift the flour on to a piece of paper. When the water boils, tip the flour in at once and stir like crazy until a ball of dough forms. Turn off the heat and continue to stir the dough for a little while until a slight film appears on the base of the saucepan. Remove from the heat and beat in each egg one at a time, making sure that each is well incorporated before you add the next. Beat well until the mixture is glossy. Leave to cool. Butter a 9 inch springform tin and chill in the freezer while you heat the oven to Gas Mark 6 (400°F, 200°C). When the oven is hot, remove the tin from the freezer and with the aid of a stiff spatula spread the choux paste over the bottom and sides of the inside of the tin as evenly as you can. This needs a little patience. Bake for about 30 minutes until well puffed and browned. Take it out of the oven and prick it in about a dozen places with a skewer to let the trapped moisture escape. Pop back into the oven, turn off the heat and leave for another 10–15 minutes to dry out. Open the door and leave until cool. It should have risen and be like a puffed-up, crisp, well-browned 'Yorkshire' pudding in appearance. It should also have shrunken away from the sides of the tin. Take out of the oven, release the clips in the side of the tin and leave on a rack to cool completely.

The Filling and Dressing

> 3 good cups of cooked chicken, cut into bite-sized pieces
> 250 grams (9 oz) of water chestnuts, drained and sliced
> 6 spring onions, thinly sliced diagonally
> 2 hard-boiled eggs, roughly chopped
> Salt and pepper
> 1 cup sour cream
> 1 teaspoon lemon or lime juice
> 2 teaspoons castor sugar
> 2 teaspoons curry powder
> 4 tablespoons mayonnaise
> Lettuce leaves or young spinach to line the pastry case
> A little chopped parsley

Put the chicken, water chestnuts, spring onions and eggs into a large bowl, season with a little pepper and salt, and toss lightly. Combine the sour cream, lemon or lime juice, castor sugar, curry powder and mayonnaise in another smaller bowl and whisk together. Pour over the chicken, mix carefully together, cover and chill. Wash and pat dry enough salad leaves to completely line the inside of the pastry case, dry and chill until ready to serve. Remove the pastry shell from the tin and place on a serving plate. Line very well, making sure that the salad leaves overlap. Spoon the chilled chicken filling on to the leaves and sprinkle with a little chopped parsley. Cut into wedges to serve.

ROAST CHICKEN WITH GARLIC CLOVES
Serves 4–6

This really is very simple and very delicious. When you cook garlic in this manner the flavour is tempered and not harsh in any way. This makes an ideal middle course for an informal lunch. When you have cooked the dish you carve the chicken into serving portions and then squeeze out the centres from the garlic cloves and spread on slices of toasted French bread to eat with the chicken. Together with a lovely fresh green salad and some cheese and fruit, you end up with a very relaxed and informal meal.

> *1 large roasting chicken*
> *Juice of two lemons*
> *1 tablespoon virgin olive oil*
> *Freshly ground black pepper*
> *2–3 heads good garlic*
> *$\frac{1}{2}$ cup water*

Truss the rinsed and dried chicken and place in a fairly large baking dish. Pour over the lemon juice and occasionally baste with the lemon juice for about 1 hour. Tip off any excess juice and rub the chicken with the olive oil all over. Sprinkle liberally with fresh black pepper. Break the garlic into cloves and place around the chicken in the baking dish and pour in the water. Roast at Gas Mark 7 (425°F, 220°C) for about 1–1½ hours, depending on the size of the chicken. Place the chicken and garlic cloves on a warm serving platter and proceed to eat as described above.

ENDS

FRUIT YORKSHIRE PUDDING
Serves 6

This sounds a little strange and is based on a French dish which makes use of soft summer fruits. We suggest stoned fresh cherries, but you may use other fresh fruit such as apples, peaches, apricots etc., which can be cut into fairly thick slices after peeling and either coring or de-seeding. Make sure that the fruits used are ripe, but not over ripe as they are cooked in the batter for about 30 minutes and over-ripe fruit would collapse too much. The sugar content can be more than we have given, according to the natural sweetness of the chosen fruit, but rather than increase it at cooking stage we serve castor sugar in a bowl or shaker to use at table in case that extra sweetness is required. A dish of either whipped cream or ice cream is another extra.

- *750 grams (1¾ lb) stoned black cherries or alternative fruit*
- *3 large eggs*
- *3 tablespoons plain flour*
- *Pinch salt*
- *6 tablespoons castor sugar*
- *2 cups milk*
- *2 tablespoons dark rum or appropriate flavoured liqueur*
- *3 tablespoons unsalted butter*

Beat the eggs together in a bowl and sift in the flour and salt. Add 4 tablespoons of the sugar and mix in well. Heat the milk to lukewarm and pour onto the egg mixture, whisking all the while until you have a batter. Stir in the rum or liqueur. Butter a wide shallow ovenproof dish and place the cherries or fruit into it. Pour over the batter and dot with the butter. Bake at Gas Mark 6 (400°F, 200°C) for about 25–30 minutes or until the edges are a golden brown. Remove from the oven and sprinkle with the remaining sugar. Serve lukewarm, not hot.

NOTE   The obvious alternative liqueurs are kirsch with cherries, calvados with apples, peach schnapps with peaches.

MIXED FRUIT FLAN
Serves 8

We humbly submit this simple but good standby so that we can include our recipe for a really good Rich Shortcrust Pastry. We often mix the fruits and depending on the season make use of both fresh and tinned. Most flans are usually filled with a pastry cream but this simple cream-cheese filling is much easier and does a lot to enhance the flavours of most fruits. As pastry is not very nice when served cold, we chill all the fruits in small dishes separately, plus the cheese filling, and then put it together just an hour before we start receiving guests. To stop the bananas discolouring we slice them into a bowl containing a few tablespoons of water and the juice of a lemon.

Let us start with the pastry that can be made either by hand in the conventional 'rubbing in' method or for real speed and ease, in a food processor.

Rich Shortcrust Pastry

> 2 cups plain flour
> Good pinch salt
> 3 tablespoons icing sugar
> 150 grams (5 oz) butter
> 1 large egg yolk
> 2–4 tablespoons chilled water

By hand   Sift the flour, salt and icing sugar into a large mixing bowl. Make sure the butter is slightly softened and rub it in with your fingers or cut in with a pastry blender. The latter, if you have one, is good because it keeps your hot hands out of the mix. Beat the egg yolk together with the water and sprinkle over the flour mixture. Mix together with a dull knife or spatula, quickly knead into a ball, place in clingwrap and pop into the fridge for at least 45 minutes.

By food processor   Place the flour, salt and icing sugar into the bowl of the food processor fitted with the steel blade, pulse on and off. Make sure the butter is well chilled and cut it into cubes, and add to the flour. Run the processor until you reach a crumb-like stage. With the motor running pour in the beaten egg yolk and 2 tablespoons of chilled water and run the motor until the dough forms a ball or until most of the mixture does. Don't be tempted to add too much water. Sometimes it is a good idea to pulse the mixture once you have added the egg and water until the ball stage is reached. Tip out the dough and quickly knead into a ball, cover and chill as above.

To bake blind   Roll the pastry out on a lightly floured surface large enough to fit the flan dish you are going to use, in this case about a 10 inch round. Gently press in the pastry over the bottom and up the sides, but under no circumstances stretch the pastry. Prick all over the base with a fork, trim the edges and again chill. Set the oven to Gas Mark 7 (425°F, 220°C). When the oven is at the right temperature, remove the pastry case from the fridge and line with a large piece of foil, making sure it extends up the sides and over the edge to protect the edges when cooking. Line the foil with either dry beans, rice or special pellets that you can buy; the first two suggestions are cheaper and if kept solely for this purpose can be used over and over again. Place in the oven and cook for 12 minutes. Lower the heat to Gas Mark 4 (350°F, 180°C) and cook for a further 10–15 minutes, carefully removing the foil and the 'weights' for the last 5 minutes to allow the base to dry out and cook. Cool and then proceed to fill with the cream-cheese filling, the fruit and finally the glaze.

Mixed Fruit Flan

One baked shortcrust pastry shell
120 grams (4½ oz) cream cheese, softened
1 teaspoon finely grated lemon rind
3 tablespoons icing sugar
2 tablespoons cream
½ cup mandarin segments, either fresh or tinned
1 large banana, sliced
½ cup cherries, either fresh or tinned
½ cup seedless white grapes
6 small apricot halves, either fresh or tinned
6 fresh strawberries, halved
1 cup apricot jam or conserve
2 tablespoons water or white port

Beat together the cream cheese, lemon rind, icing sugar and cream to a soft spreading consistency; you may need to add a little extra cream. Spread this over the base of the cooked flan case when ready to assemble. Remove pith and pips from fresh mandarin segments, stone the cherries, or drain tinned fruit. Place all the fruit on top in circles to make an eye-catching arrangement. Place the apricot jam, water or port in a small saucepan and heat until runny, strain through a sieve and spoon the resulting glaze over the fruit. Serve with lightly sweetened cream if you wish.

TARTE TATIN
Serves 8

This is much richer than the normal apple pie and is a French Classic. We devised the recipe for the pastry after a lot of trial runs and now it is very good indeed. As this is started on top of the stove and then transferred to the oven we strongly suggest that you use a good heavy frying-pan that has a handle that won't burn. Many of the heavy cast-iron types that are enamelled are good for this. We did try it in a tin once but it wasn't easy to get the finished result out. We also serve this with a particular type of cream which we include here. The cream will also go very well with fruit or other rich endings to a meal such as chocolate pudding.

Pastry

> 4 *tablespoons water*
> 1 *egg yolk*
> 1 *teaspoon bland oil*
> 2 *cups plain flour*
> 2 *tablespoons icing sugar*
> 3 *tablespoons castor sugar*
> *Pinch salt*
> 175 *grams (6 oz) butter, softened*

Mix water, egg yolk and oil together in a small jug and place in the fridge to chill. Sift flour, icing and castor sugars and salt into a large bowl and cut in the butter with a blunt knife or spatula or work in with a wire pastry blender. Then sprinkle the water and egg mixture over the dry ingredients and quickly work into a dough. Put in a plastic bag and pop in the fridge for at least an hour.

Filling

> 5 or 6 good quality eating apples, depending on size
> 100 grams (4 oz) butter
> 6 tablespoons castor sugar

Peel, core and quarter the apples and put into some cold water together with the juice of a lemon. Put the butter and sugar into your pan. Heat them together until they start to bubble slightly. Drain and dry the apples and carefully place in the pan, off the heat, arranging the slices attractively. Put the pan back on the heat and simmer until the butter-sugar mixture bubbles up between the slices of apple and then starts to caramelize. This takes about 15 minutes. Set the oven to Gas Mark 6 (400°F, 200°C). Take the apples off the heat. Roll out the chilled pastry on a lightly floured surface to a size just slightly larger than the pan, then place on top and tuck in the edges. Bake for 15–20 minutes or until the pastry is golden brown. Remove and leave to settle for about 5 minutes; then using the handle invert the whole thing on to a serving plate. Leave to cool to room temperature as it is best served warm not cold, with cream (see below).

NOTE This inverting bit isn't always easy. Run a knife around the edge of the pastry to make sure it is released from the pan. If, when you invert it, the apples don't all come out beautifully, don't panic; just take the rest out and pat back on top to look as attractive as possible. Believe us when we say that no one will notice that much and all will be forgiven anyway as the taste is magnificent.

The Cream

> 1 cup cream
> 3 tablespoons castor sugar
> $\frac{1}{4}$ teaspoon vanilla essence
> 1 small egg yolk
> 1 rounded tablespoon sour cream

Beat the cream and sugar until thick but not stiff. Add the essence, yolk and sour cream and re-beat to as stiff as you can; it won't be ultra stiff, but very thick. Cover and chill for at least 2 hours.

PEAR AND ALMOND TART
Serves 8–10

Although this recipe calls for fresh pears you can at a pinch use tinned pear halves when fresh ones are not available. If you do, boil the claret, lemon juice, sugar and cinnamon stick for 10 minutes, place the drained pear halves in the mixture and remove from the heat immediately. Allow them to stay in the liquid until cold. Don't, however, slice them when placing them on the frangipane cream or they will disintegrate.

> 5 large firm but ripe pears
> 2 cups cold water with 1 tablespoon lemon juice added
> 1¾ cups good claret
> 2 tablespoons lemon juice
> 6 tablespoons sugar
> 1 cinnamon stick
> ¼ cup redcurrant jelly
> A 10 inch fully cooked shortcrust pastry shell
> One recipe Frangipane Cream (see below)

Frangipane Cream

> 1 egg plus one egg yolk
> 5 tablespoons sugar
> 4 tablespoons plain flour
> 1¼ cups boiling milk
> 50 grams (2 oz) butter
> 2 teaspoons vanilla essence
> ¼ teaspoon almond essence
> 75 grams (3 oz) freshly ground almonds
> 2 tablespoons kirsch or pear liqueur (optional)

Make the Frangipane Cream first as it has to go cold. Beat the whole egg and the egg yolk in a large mixing bowl. Gradually beat in the sugar until thick and pale yellow. Beat in the sifted flour and then add the boiling milk in a stream, beating all the time. Rinse out the milk saucepan in cold water and pour the egg and milk mixture back into it. Cook

over moderate heat for about 2 minutes, stirring all
the time until it thickens. Don't let it burn. Remove
from the heat and beat in the remaining ingredients
and leave to go cold.

NOTE   It should not curdle because of the addition
of the flour, but we have had it burn on the odd
occasion. Press a piece of clingwrap over the surface
of the cream while it is cooling. This will stop a skin
forming.

Peel and halve the pears and remove the cores with
either a small spoon or a grapefruit knife and drop
them into the water and lemon juice to stop them
turning brown. Bring the wine, lemon juice, sugar
and cinnamon stick to the boil in either an enamel
or stainless steel saucepan. Drain the pear halves
and carefully place in the simmering wine. Simmer
for about 8 minutes or until just tender. Remove
from the heat and leave for 20 minutes, then take
out the pear halves with a slotted spoon and drain
on a rack cut-side down. Bring the wine syrup back
to the boil and boil until reduced by over a half,
about 10 minutes. In a small saucepan put the
redcurrant jelly and a quarter cup of the reduced
wine syrup. Heat together, stirring until the jelly
has dissolved. Remove from the heat and leave this
glaze to cool. Paint the inside of the cooked pastry
case with a thin layer of the redcurrant glaze and
spread over the Frangipane Cream. Slice the
poached pear halves and place decoratively over the
cream and brush the remaining redcurrant glaze
over the pears. Chill for about 2 hours.

CHOCOLATE NUT MERINGUE CAKE
Serves 8–12

This is strictly for entertaining. It takes a little time but is not difficult. Our mouths fairly quiver at the very thought of the taste of the end result. Take each stage slowly and you will finish up with a triumph. Before you start, line two swiss-roll tins with a double thickness of foil, turning up the edges all round by about 1½ inches. Butter them and dredge very lightly with cornflour, shaking off any excess, and place side by side on another flat baking sheet.

> *250 grams (9 oz) blanched almonds*
> *150 grams (5 oz) hazelnuts*
> *1½ cups castor sugar*
> *8 egg whites*
> *Pinch of salt*
> *250 grams (9 oz) cooking chocolate*
> *125 grams (4½ oz) unsalted butter*
> *1 cup cream, stiffly beaten*
> *Extra ¾ cup cream plus ½ teaspoon vanilla essence, stiffly beaten*
> *Chocolate flake or hail to decorate*
> *Icing sugar to decorate*

Spread the almonds and hazelnuts out on two separate baking trays and place in a moderate oven to brown them gently. When the almonds are lightly browned and the hazelnut skins have puckered, take them out of the oven. Remove as much of the skins from the hazelnuts as you can by rubbing them in a

dry tea-towel. When cool, grind the nuts finely and
mix with the sugar. This can be done in a food
processor, a mouli fitted with a fine blade, or a
blender. Set aside about a quarter of the nut and
sugar mixture. Beat the egg whites with a pinch of
salt until stiff, and carefully fold in three-quarters of
the nut and sugar mixture. Set the oven to Gas
Mark 6 (400°F, 200°C). Divide and spread the
meringue mixture equally between the two prepared
foil cases. Put them both on the baking sheet and
place in the pre-heated oven in the middle and cook
for about 25 to 30 minutes until crisp but not burnt.
Remove and cool on a rack. Remove the foil and
leave to go cold and then cut each one in half
lengthwise, so you have four long strips of equal
size. Break the chocolate into small pieces and place
in a bowl over a saucepan of hot water. As the
chocolate starts to melt, add the butter in small
pieces, stirring all the time. Remember that you can
only use unsalted butter. Remove from the heat
when all the butter has been amalgamated and
again leave to cool right down. Add the first cup of
whipped cream to the chocolate, stir until smooth
and chill. Into the second lot of cream and vanilla,
stir the reserved quarter of nuts and sugar, and
chill. Place one of the meringue strips on a serving
plate and cover with a quarter of the chocolate
cream. Place the second meringue strip on top and
cover with all the nut cream mixture. Place the
third strip of meringue on top of this layer and again
cover with a quarter of the chocolate cream. Place
the final strip of meringue on top and spread the
remaining chocolate cream around the sides of the

cake. Pat on some of the chocolate flake or hail around the sides of the cake to cover the cream. Do this with the aid of a broad spatula. With the remaining chocolate flake and icing sugar make a decorative pattern on top of the cake. Diagonal lines about an inch and a half wide are effective and fairly easy. Chill for several hours before serving.

NOTE You can trim up the edges of the meringues once they are cooked to give an even shape, before filling and covering the sides. A good idea is to lay the meringue on a large sheet of greaseproof paper so that once you have completely decorated it you can take off any excess chocolate flake and then place it on a clean serving dish. Personally we just blow them off!

CREAM NUT RING
Serves 6–8

This consists of a pastry ring made from choux pastry, a simple cream filling and a glaze of caramelized sugar. The secret of choux pastry is to cook it until crisp. This means that it stays in the oven for possibly longer than one would imagine and we have had constant fights about when to bring it out; but trust us – we know what we are doing. The recipe is divided up into three parts: the choux pastry ring first; the filling; and then the topping. The topping you have to do fairly close to the time of serving, for once it is on you cannot then put the Cream Nut Ring back in the fridge otherwise it won't stay crisp.

Choux Pastry

> 30 grams (1 oz) butter
> 1 teaspoon castor sugar
> ¾ cup milk
> 1¼ cups plain flour
> 3 large eggs

Filling

> 3 tablespoons slivered almonds
> 1¼ cups cream
> 3 tablespoons vanilla sugar

Glaze

> 6 tablespoons sugar
> 4 tablespoons water

To prepare the choux pastry put the butter, sugar and milk into a saucepan and slowly bring to the boil, stirring to make sure that the sugar is dissolved. Sift the flour on to a piece of paper and when the milk starts to boil tip it in all at once and remove the saucepan from the heat. Stir like crazy to incorporate the flour with a wooden spoon. Beat the eggs into the paste one at a time; this is not easy, but they must be well incorporated before the next is beaten in. Now set the oven to Gas Mark 6 (400°F, 200°C). Place the pastry mix into a forcing bag fitted with a fairly large plain nozzle and pipe a circle on to a lightly buttered baking tray about 1½ inches thick and 8 inches in diameter. If you don't have a forcing bag then cut the corner, not too big, from a plastic bag and use that, or failing either, dollop spoonfuls of the mixture into a circle and pat together with the back of a wetted spoon. Bake in the middle of the oven for 30 minutes, turn off the heat and leave for a further 10 minutes. Finally leave the oven door ajar and leave for another 10 minutes. The colour will be very dark but it should not be burnt. Remove and leave to cool then split in half horizontally and remove any uncooked dough so that both halves of the ring are hollow, leaving a crust.

Toast the slivered almonds on a metal tray in a moderate oven until golden brown and leave to cool. Whip the cream and vanilla sugar together until fairly stiff, fold in the cold toasted slivered almonds and place in the base of the ring. Fill the bottom half full so that it is mounded up, place the top on and pop in the fridge while you make the glaze.

In a small saucepan bring the sugar and water to the boil for the glaze and boil until it turns and smells of caramel. Remove the ring from the fridge and quickly pour the caramel glaze over the top. You have to do this quickly as it sets almost immediately. Serve straight away by cracking through the topping and then slicing through the ring base.

NOTE   After you have poured over the glaze you can return it to the fridge prior to serving but for no longer than an hour, otherwise the glaze reverts to a liquid. Then let stand at room temperature for about 30 minutes before cutting.

COLD LEMON CARAMEL SOUFFLÉ
Serves 4

As this has a sharpish sweet taste it is an ideal ending to a rich meal. A lot of people hate the time taken to thicken eggs over the top of a double boiler, but believe us the extra time involved does give a better end result. If you want to ring the changes slightly we suggest using fresh lime juice rather than the lemon, in which case you will need the juice from two small limes. When you have made the caramel and you add the extra water, do be careful that it doesn't spatter over you.

> 6 *tablespoons castor sugar*
> 4 *tablespoons water, plus 4 more*
> 1 *tablespoon gelatin*
> *Juice of 1 lemon plus 3 tablespoons warm water*
> 2 *large eggs separated plus an extra yolk*
> 3 *tablespoons castor sugar*
> $\frac{1}{2}$ *cup cream, softly whipped*

Put the 6 tablespoons of castor sugar and 4 tablespoons of water into a medium-sized saucepan and bring to the boil. Keep simmering until the mixture turns a darkish caramel colour. You can tell when it has by the caramel smell. Remove from the heat and carefully add 4 more tablespoons of water to the pan, stir and put to one side. Sprinkle the gelatin over the lemon juice and water mixture and leave to soften. Place the egg yolks and the 3 tablespoons sugar in the top of a double saucepan and whisk. Add the gelatin and lemon mixture and cook over simmering water until the mixture thickens, whisking all the time or stirring with a wooden spoon. When the mixture has thickened, take off the heat and add the cooled caramel mixture. Leave to cool, stirring occasionally. Whip the 2 egg whites until stiff and fold into the cold egg-yolk mixture, then fold in the beaten cream. Pour into four small dishes and chill for at least 3 hours.

LIGHT APPLE PUDDING
Serves 4–6

When making either mayonnaise or crème brulée you often end up with several egg whites. These, of course, can be whipped up into a meringue, but you don't always fancy something that sweet. Here is a good way of using them. You can freeze egg whites satisfactorily, but make sure you note how many you have frozen in one batch and also leave them to come back to room temperature before attempting to whip them. This dish is just a little richer than the normal apple snow.

> $2\frac{1}{4}$ cups apple purée, fresh preferably but tinned can be used
>
> 1 tablespoon powdered gelatin

Juice of 1 lemon
Castor sugar to sweeten if required
2 egg whites, stiffly beaten
½ cup cream, whipped to soft peaks
Extra whipped cream to decorate

If the apple is not sweetened do so with some castor sugar after you have added the gelatin and lemon juice, but keep it on the sharp side because you want it to taste refreshing. Pour the lemon juice into a small bowl and sprinkle the gelatin over the top. Either melt by placing that bowl in some hot water, stirring until the gelatin has dissolved, or pop it in the microwave for about 45 seconds on full power. Stir into the apple purée. Pop into the fridge to chill but not to set. Fold in the beaten egg whites, then gently fold in the cream. With a spatula put the mixture into a dish or mould, previously rinsed in cold water or into individual serving glasses. Chill for at least 3 hours. Serve decorated with swirls of whipped cream.

SWEET AVOCADO PIE
Serves 8–10

We are all fairly familiar with avocados served with a seafood filling or mashed into guacamole or even with vinaigrette but we don't often use them as an end to a meal. This recipe is ideal when you can get avocados that are sometimes slightly damaged very cheaply, although you must not use any parts of the flesh that are discoloured. You may mash the avocado if you wish, but a food processor gives a much smoother result.

Crumb Crust

> 1½ cups finely crushed plain biscuit crumbs
> ¼ cup very finely chopped almonds
> ¼ cup castor sugar
> ¼ cup melted butter

Mix well together all the ingredients and press over the base and up the sides of a 9 inch loose-bottomed tin. Bake at Gas Mark 3 (325°F, 170°C) for 10 minutes. Remove from the oven and allow to cool.

Avocado Filling

> 3 egg yolks, beaten
> 1 tin sweetened condensed milk, about 400 grams
> 2 large ripe avocados
> ½ cup lemon juice
> 1 teaspoon finely grated lemon rind
> 1 cup sour cream
> 1 teaspoon vanilla essence
> 1 tablespoon castor sugar

Combine the beaten egg yolks and condensed milk in a medium-sized saucepan and cook, stirring constantly over moderate heat until thickened. Leave to cool, stirring now and then. Process the avocados, together with the lemon juice and peel, until smooth. Now add the cooled milk and egg mixture and again process until combined. Pour into the cooled pie crust and chill for at least an hour. Mix well the sour cream, vanilla and sugar until the sugar has dissolved and smooth the mixture over the top of the avocado filling. Chill until set, at least 3 hours. The centre will be slightly soft when you cut it.

PUMPKIN PIE
Serves 6–8

You can steam some fresh pumpkin and purée in a food processor, or failing that mash it. However, if the latter it must be really smooth. You can also buy tinned puréed pumpkin. If you have never served pumpkin as a sweet dish before, don't tell your guests . . . they will eat it and surely love it. You will need to have a 9 inch fairly deep pie dish, round, lined with pastry and in the fridge before you start to make this. Preferably a sweet shortcrust.

> *One 9 inch shortcrust uncooked pastry shell*
> *8 tablespoons cream*
> *8 tablespoons milk*
> *180 grams (6 oz) soft dark brown sugar*
> *1 teaspoon cinnamon*
> *$\frac{1}{8}$ teaspoon ground cloves*
> *$\frac{1}{2}$ teaspoon powdered ginger*
> *3 eggs, lightly beaten*
> *2 tablespoons calvados or brandy*
> *250 grams (9 oz) puréed pumpkin*

In a large mixing bowl whisk together the cream, milk, sugar, cinnamon, cloves and ginger. Stir in the beaten eggs, calvados or brandy and the puréed pumpkin. Carefully pour the filling into the chilled pie shell and bake at Gas Mark 3 (325°F, 170°C) for 40 to 50 minutes in the middle of the oven until the centre of the pie just quivers when jiggled from side to side. It will finish cooking when you remove it from the oven and leave it to come to room temperature before serving. Do not chill it as the flavour is not the same as when served at room temperature.

NOTE   We find that as the pie shell is uncooked to start with, place a metal oven tray or sheet in the oven while it is heating up, then place the pie on this to cook. The extra heat generated by the metal tray helps cook the base of the pie.

NECTARINES IN VODKA
Serves 6

Everything about this recipe must be at the peak of perfection for it to really taste its best. The nectarines must be really ripe and the grapes must be of the seedless variety. You can make this the morning of the day on which it is going to be served, but unfortunately it will not keep for the next day if there is any left over as the nectarines darken and it looks unattractive. Chill the glasses in which you are going to serve this to your guests and frost the rims if you wish by dipping each rim into lightly beaten egg white then into a bowl or saucer of castor sugar.

> 2 cups thinly sliced nectarines
> 1 cup seedless green grapes
> $\frac{1}{4}$ cup vodka
> $\frac{1}{4}$ cup freshly squeezed orange juice
> 2 tablespoons castor sugar
> 2 tablespoons freshly grated orange rind
> 1 tablespoon finely chopped candied ginger

Place the prepared nectarines and grapes into an attractive serving bowl, preferably glass. Mix the remaining ingredients together and pour over. Carefully mix together with a large spoon, cover and chill until ready to serve. Stir them occasionally to get all the flavours well mixed together.

NOTE You may do the same thing with ripe fresh peaches that have been peeled before slicing. You can then change the vodka to a few tablespoons of peach schnapps instead.

CHOCOLATE RUM MOUSSE
Serves 4

There is always room for one chocolate dessert and this is possibly the simplest and most delicious. It is best made the day before you require it. The addition of the butter, which must be unsalted, gives the final result a certain roundness. Once you have completed this basic recipe you can add to it $\frac{1}{2}$ cup of cream whipped fairly stiff and folded in at the end for a softer lighter taste. You can also add the finely grated rind of 1 orange and if you wish a tablespoon of orange liqueur to the original. The liqueur is optional as the orange rind is sufficient to give it that delicate orange flavour.

> *200 grams (7 oz) of dark chocolate*
> *3 tablespoons hot water*
> *1 rounded teaspoon of instant coffee powder*
> *1 tablespoon of unsalted butter*
> *2 tablespoons dark rum*
> *3 large eggs separated*

Break the chocolate into small pieces and melt in a basin over a pot of simmering water or in the microwave. Mix the water and coffee powder together until dissolved and stir into the chocolate. Remove from the heat source. Stir in the butter and the rum and mix thoroughly; we use a spatula which makes it easier to scrape out later into pots. Stir in the lightly beaten egg yolks and when thoroughly incorporated, fold in the stiffly beaten egg whites. Divide equally between 4 glasses or bowls and place in the fridge to set, preferably overnight.

DOLCE ALLA PIEMONTESE
Serves 6–8

This can be made up to a certain stage several days in advance and then frozen until ready to complete and serve. It is the sort of ending to a meal that even people who have a tendency not to eat sweet things rave over. For it you need to make a pastry cream, which can also be used in other ways. For example, you can use it to line the base of a cooked sweet pastry case, before topping with fruit and then a glaze, to make a lovely flan, or you can fill small profiteroles or cream puffs with it. If you don't want to go to the trouble of making the pastry cream you can make a thick version of a commercial custard powder with the addition of some finely grated lemon peel added to it. For this dish save some egg whites to make the meringue covering.

> 1 recipe of pastry cream (or custard – see above)
> made in advance
> 1 oblong madeira cake, homemade or bought
> 2 tablespoons cointreau
> 1 heaped tablespoon bitter orange marmalade
> 5 egg whites
> 8 tablespoons castor sugar
> Extra castor and icing sugars to dust

Pastry Cream

> 1 cup milk
> 2 tablespoons castor sugar
> ½ teaspoon vanilla essence

3 *tablespoons plain flour*
2 *egg yolks*
Finely grated rind of one lemon
1 *tablespoon butter*

Start by making the pastry cream as it has to be chilled before using. Slowly bring the milk up to boiling point. Place the egg yolks into a medium-sized bowl together with the sugar, and whisk until thick and creamy. When whisked enough, you can lift it out and make a trail across with the mixture that falls from the whisk. This should remain there for a few seconds before disappearing back into the mixture. Whisk in the flour and the lemon rind until well combined and then gradually whisk in the boiling milk. Rinse out the saucepan in cold water and return the mixture to it. Re-heat, stirring all the time until the mixture boils up once. Remove from the heat and beat in the butter, cool. Place a piece of clingwrap to cover the surface of the pastry cream. This will help prevent a thick skin forming on top.

Split the madeira cake lengthwise in half and place on an ovenproof serving dish. Sprinkle half the liqueur over the cut surface. Spread with the marmalade. Now spread with the cold pastry cream (or custard) and place the second half of the cake on top. Sprinkle with the remainder of the liqueur. Place in the freezer until chilled, or freeze until required, as mentioned at the beginning of the recipe. We strongly recommend that you anchor the cake with several long toothpicks or thin metal skewers so that it doesn't accidentally slide apart.

These can be removed if the cake is frozen prior to piping with the meringue mixture.

Whisk the egg whites until stiff and add half the sugar, whisk again until really stiff and glossy. Fold in the other half of the sugar and place into a piping bag fitted with a ½inch plain nozzle. Pipe all around the cake in uprights and finish off the top with mushroom-like blobs. The cake surface must be covered completely. Sprinkle liberally with extra castor sugar and bake in the lower centre of the oven pre-heated to Gas Mark 2 (300°F, 160°C) until the whole thing is a light golden brown, about 20 to 30 minutes. Remove to cool, not in the fridge, and when cold, dust all over liberally with icing sugar.

NOTE   Don't do what we did on television and have the heat too high to try to cook it quicker: it goes 'burnt black' not golden brown.

CHOCOLATE AND MARSALA CREAM
Serves 6–8

This is very similar to Zabaione but is lighter and served cold. As the end result is fairly rich it goes a long way and is very good to end a meal that has been fairly light. Two things to remember are to have the eggs at room temperature before starting, and not to boil the water but simmer and don't let it touch the base of either the bowl or the top of a double boiler, whichever you choose to use. We personally never keep eggs in the fridge, but rather in a wire egg basket somewhere cool. This cream can be served in a soufflé dish or in individual glasses; we prefer the latter.

> 4 *eggs, separated*
> $\frac{1}{2}$ *cup castor sugar*
> $\frac{1}{2}$ *cup marsala*
> 1 *tablespoon powdered gelatin softened in 4 table-spoons water*
> 1 *cup cream whipped fairly stiff*
> 4 *tablespoons grated milk chocolate, more if desired*
> Extra *whipped cream and grated chocolate for decoration*

Beat egg yolks and sugar together in a bowl over hot water or in the top of a double boiler. Whisk over simmering water for several minutes then add the marsala and continue to cook until the mixture thickens. Don't rush this or scrambled eggs will result. When thickened, add the gelatin mixture, remove from the heat and continue mixing till the gelatin has dissolved. Cool the mixture, stirring now and again. When cool, fold in the whipped cream and grated chocolate. Whip the egg whites until stiff, fold in about a quarter to lighten the mixture then fold in the remainder. Pour into dish or glasses and chill for at least 2 hours. Decorate the top with whipped cream and grated chocolate.

CRÊPES WITH COINTREAU SAUCE
Serves 4

You can use your savoury crêpes that you have
stored in the freezer for this recipe or you might like
to make a batch of crêpes specifically for dessert use.
If you do then add 2 tablespoons of cognac and 2
tablespoons of castor sugar to the original crêpe
batter. Should you not want to use the liqueur in
this recipe then add the equivalent in extra orange
juice. If you have a table-top chafing dish and burner
then use it to impress your guests; failing that, just
use your favourite large pan in the kitchen. These
are best served straight away rather than made
ahead of time and re-heated.

> 8 cooked crêpes
> 2 tablespoons butter
> 3 tablespoons sugar
> Finely grated rind and juice of 1 orange
> Juice of half a lemon
> $\frac{1}{3}$ cup cointreau

Fold each crêpe into quarters by folding in half,
then half again to form a wedge shape. Put butter
and sugar in the pan and heat until the butter melts
and bubbles. Stir in the juice and rind of the orange
and the lemon juice and bring to the boil, stirring
all the time. Lower the heat slightly and add the
cointreau, keeping the sauce hot but not boiling.
Dip each folded crêpe into the sauce, turning after
30 seconds, and then with a pair of tongs transfer
to a warm lipped serving dish. When all the crêpes

have been dipped bring the remaining sauce to
the boil and pour over the crêpes. Serve straight
away.

NOTE You may serve some stiffly beaten cream or
a small scoop of vanilla ice cream if you wish.

BANANA AND RUM PIE
Serves 8

If you are definitely on a diet then you can forget
this now. However if you want to treat yourself and
guests to a rather super end to a meal after something light there really could be nothing easier than
this recipe. Make sure that the bananas are ripe
but still firm as they are to be cooked slightly. You
need not serve this with whipped cream, although
the appearance of the pie without the cream topping doesn't look as attractive. However, flavour
is there. It was one of our standbys in our restaurant days and like a lot of things we did, had it's
regular devotees who would ask for it every time
they came in. We had one person who almost burst
into tears once when we had to explain that we had
sold out.

One 9 inch baked short pastry shell
6 bananas
¼ cup liquid honey
3 tablespoons soft brown sugar
Freshly grated nutmeg

2 tablespoons dark rum
2 tablespoons butter
Plenty of sweetened whipped cream

Slice the bananas into diagonal slices, about ¾ inch thick, into a large bowl. Drizzle over the honey and mix. Sprinkle over the sugar, grated nutmeg (about a quarter of a whole one) and add the rum and again mix altogether. Mound into the baked pastry shell and dot with the butter. Bake at Gas Mark 5 (375°F, 190°C) for about 15 minutes. Remove and leave to go cold. Pile on the whipped cream and smooth over the bananas. Chill for a little while and serve.

NOTE   Just before adding the cream you might like to drizzle over some lime or lemon juice to give the whole thing a zing.

CHAMPAGNE AND ORANGE SORBET
Serves 8

This not only makes for a refreshing break after a middle course at either dinner or lunch, but can be a perfect end to practically any meal. The quantity is sufficient for eight people to end a meal with more if only a small amount is served as a palate refresher. Having experimented with this many times, we have made it in an ice cream machine that has a paddle which turns while the mixture is freezing. But you can put it in the freezer in a metal container and mash it up just prior to serving. Either way it tastes the same. As there is a lot of alcohol and sugar it usually doesn't set that hard so it's best served straight from the freezer and in chilled glasses. The balance of the champagne can be a treat for the cook or the remains of the bottle can be used in the Champagne and Pumpkin Sauce that accompanies the Chicken Parcels (see page 120). A final tip: we have found that soft brown sugar instead of white sugar gives an indefinable taste to the end result.

$\frac{1}{2}$ *cup soft brown sugar*
$\frac{1}{4}$ *cup water*
Juice of a lemon, plus the thinly pared rind
Juice of an orange, plus the finely grated rind
Dry champagne

Bring the water and sugar to the boil in a small saucepan together with the thinly pared lemon rind and boil for 5 minutes. Remove from the heat and leave to cool. Strain this syrup through a sieve into a measuring jug when cool and add the strained juice of the lemon and orange. Make up to 1 litre (4 cups) with the champagne, pouring in the champagne slowly and stir as it froths up. Chill the liquid, stir in the orange rind and then freeze either in an ice-cream-making machine, following the manufacturer's times, or place into a metal tin and freeze until firm in your freezer. Spoon into chilled glasses when ready to serve.

INDEX